FURNACE OF THE HEART

FURNACE OF THE HEART

Rekindling our Longing
for God

Sr Margaret Magdalen CSMV

DARTON·LONGMAN + TODD

First published in 1998 by
Darton, Longman and Todd Ltd
1 Spencer Court
140–142 Wandsworth High Street
London SW18 4JJ

ISBN 0–232–52243–X

A catalogue record for this book is available
from the British Library

Thanks are due to the following for permission
to quote copyright material:

Oxford University Press for prayer by George Appleton, taken from
The Oxford Book of Prayer (© 1985); SCM Press for 'Christians and
Pagans', *Letters and Papers from Prison* by Dietrich Bonhoeffer, The
Enlarged Edition (© 1997); SLG Press for prayer by Sister Ruth, taken
from *The Oxford Book of Prayer*; SPCK for *All Desires Known* by Janet Morley
and *Guru and Disciple* translated by Heather Sandeman; Wild Goose
Publications for prayers by Kathy Galloway and Alison Adam taken
from *Pattern of Our Days: Liturgies and Resources for Worship*, edited by
Kathy Galloway (© 1996).

Designed by Sandie Boccacci
Phototypeset in 11/14.5pt Joanna by Intype London Ltd
Printed and bound in Great Britain by
Redwood Books, Trowbridge, Wiltshire

Dedicated to Helena, Marjorie, Sylvia, Pam, Jane, Kerry,

Contents

Acknowledgements

My heartfelt thanks go to the many who have helped me in the venture of writing this book: to Morag Reeve, Editorial Director of Darton, Longman and Todd, for her gentle but persistent prompting without which I would never have ventured to write at all; to Bishop David and Carol Beetge, and Kate, who once again offered me very generous hospitality and the freedom of their home with the space, solitude and silence in which to write; to William Neill-Hall, my agent; to Daphne Shields for the immense task of typing up a handwritten manuscript, and for all the patience that involved; to the Revd Gavin Sklar-Chik who first suggested the theme of this book to me and read it in manuscript form; to my brother, Peter Evening, for researching and providing most of the quotations for Chapter 7; to the Revd Jane Richards, Sr Mildred Rebecca CSMV and the Revd Trevor Hudson for reading the manuscript, responding with much needed and appreciated encouragement, and for their very helpful suggestions; to Sr Liz Elbert OP for her sharing, criticisms and inspiration; to Stevie Ancient for practical support; to Pauline Jackson, Zohra Pillay and Ian Thomson, of the High Veld Diocesan Staff, for practical help, especially when I struggled with an ailing computer-printer!; to Mother Barbara Claire CSMV and Sr Gillian Ruth CSMV for their help in searching for references; to Helena Schüssel for her art work; to my brother Martin Evening, for photographic work.

I am especially indebted to James Houston, Gerald May, Eugene Peterson and Ronald Rolheiser, whose thinking both stimulated and chimed in with much of my own, and very grateful to them for allowing me to quote them fairly extensively.

Lastly, I must thank all those who, without my being aware of it, have been instrumental in bringing this book to birth – the authors of spiritual classics who, especially during my years as a Sister, have been 'forming' and influencing my own spirituality and whose thinking and writing may well be reflected in what I have written; the many friends who have supported me in prayer, interest and encouragement . . . especially my Sisters of the Community of St Mary the Virgin here in South Africa.

And to any others who have been part of this enterprise, and whom I have unwittingly failed to acknowledge, I offer my very sincere thanks and apologies.

Margaret Magdalen CSMV
Brakpan
R.S.A.

As Moses in the bush aflame
First heard the mystery of God's Name,
We in the furnace of Thy heart
Behold, O Jesus, what Thou art.

Heart of our God, and our desire
Strike from our flint Thy spark of fire.
Give us yet more that gift unpriced,
A share in Thy compassion, Christ.

Taken from a hymn for the Feast of the Sacred Heart,
written by Sr Janet CSMV,
from the Daily Office (of CSMV and CSP).
Copyright CSMV.

Preface

It was after one of our regular sessions of sharing in spiritual direction that a friend said to me, 'You know – whenever we meet, you always end up talking about longing for God. I reckon it is the crux of your spirituality. You ought to write a book on the subject!'

He had sowed a seed. I watered it in prayer – it would not go away, so I decided I was meant to pursue it further.

Before I left England for South Africa, Morag Reeve of Darton, Longman and Todd had pleaded first option on my next book. So, I sent her an outline of suggested chapter headings and received an enthusiastic response and encouragement to 'go ahead'. The Reverend Mother of our Community gave me permission to write – if I could find the time – and so the book was launched.

Over the years, I have given a number of retreats on this subject, and much of the material from those retreat addresses has been incorporated into this book. But, by doing so, I was faced with a major dilemma. When writing retreat addresses, I do not automatically include in my notes full details of the sources of the quotations I am using, since that would be disruptive to the flow of the address. But, wherever possible, I tell the retreatants the *author* of the quotations. However, in using material originally written some years ago, I have been unable always to remember the titles of the books, their publication dates and page numbers and even in a few cases the name of the author. For this I apologise most sincerely. Even so, I have been reluctant to omit these quotations because in most cases they are absolute 'gems'. I have done my best to trace all the references but can only beg the reader's indulgence where I have failed. We absorb so much in our reading that gradually becomes a part of us, and part of our accumulated knowledge, that at times it is difficult to distinguish between an original thought and what we may have 'picked up' along the way. If, by chance, I have confused the two in this book, I can only plead the power of the word to stay with one, to give ongoing nourishment and stimulation to thinking. Since all our creativity, including creative writing, is from God, we can really only thank the Holy Spirit who prompts the thoughts in the first place and breathes life into them so that they bring about spiritual growth in others.

I have tried in the following chapters to explore the nature of longings and have asserted that each of us is born with an innate longing for the God in whose image we are made and who, in turn, longs for our companionship. Our hearts are indeed restless until they find their rest in him, as Augustine said. There is in each of us a God-shaped gap which only he can fill – whether or not we recognise it. It is a universal longing which expresses itself in a vast variety of forms of worship.

Since, however, we have a great confusion of longings, some of which we would be ashamed to admit to, we need to sift and sort them – to discard or reject those that are not life-giving and enhancing, to cultivate those that are. In order to do that, we have to face our illusions, however painful that may be. But first, we have to acknowledge that we *have* illusions before we can undergo the necessary disillusionment.

It is often difficult to give shape and form to our longings – they are just vaguely there gnawing away at us. It is even more difficult at times to express them in words or images. This is particularly true of our deepest longings – for God. So it seemed important to include a chapter on the language of longing, since this presents a real difficulty to some.

People are often puzzled, indeed deeply distressed, by the periods of darkness and aridity which, although painful and frightening, are actually normal to any healthy spiritual life. *Why* does God appear to play games with us, absent himself when we most need him, and remain silent when we are desperate to hear him speak *some* word? Part of the exploration of this book, then, has been to discover some of the reasons for what feels like deprivation and a 'toying' with our longings.

Longing for God and sharing in his suffering are inseparable. He asks us to be 'partners in his pain', and we need both to understand what is happening when we are drawn into that divine sorrow and also to recognise the privilege of sharing in the compassion of Christ.

All our longings like our motives are mixed. But when

they have been pruned and purified, we shall at last reach the point where we can say that God alone is what we long for – not what he can give us, or make us – but him for his own sake.

The book concludes with a quarry of quotations to help those who find the written word a 'way in' to that nourishing, contemplative silence where we are never satisfied but strangely drawn into ever deeper relationship with him who is the source and goal of all our longings. Sometimes the longings gestate within us for years. We simply need a 'midwife' to help bring them to birth, so that we can name them, love them and recognise them. It is hoped that the quotations here will serve to do that for at least *some* of the readers of this book.

ONE

DEEP CALLS TO DEEP[1]
The Nature of Longing

Our restless spirits yearn for Thee,
Where e'er our changeful lot is cast.
Glad when Thy gracious smile we see,
Blest when our faith can hold Thee fast.

Latin, twelfth century, trans. R. Palmer

God doth not want a perfect work only an infinite desire.

Catherine of Siena

The restless heart

My parents, who were pioneer missionaries, returned
with my brother for a furlough from what was then the
Belgian Congo, and shortly after their arrival in England,
I was born. After only three months, my father had to
go back to help sort out a crisis in the mission. My
mother remained until my brother and I could be
admitted to a Home for Missionaries' Children where
we would be brought up by two remarkable ladies (who
became our Guardians) and a team of two or three
helpers. Not surprisingly, the staff of the Home was
reluctant to encourage the trauma of separation at only
three months, so our mother stayed with us till I was
nearly ten months old. My brother was just a year and

1

two weeks older than I. Being so young, neither of us could remember clearly our parents' faces after their departure, yet we were constantly made aware of their existence and their love by all that our Guardians told us about them, by the photo that each of us had by our bed and which we always kissed 'Good night', and by the letters that arrived (beautifully illustrated). Throughout our early years, we were often encouraged and complimented for anything good that we did with words such as, 'Won't Mummy and Daddy be proud of you!' or, 'Mummy and Daddy will be so pleased to see what a big girl/boy you have become and how grown up you are!' It was strange how being 'grown up' seemed to be held out as the great goal of our childhood!

Our greatest longing, as the years went by, was for that day when our parents would return. We looked forward to it eagerly, preparing for it by trying to excel at all manner of things, aiming to be the kind of children of whom they could be proud. And, in a way, the efforts and achievements were not for their own sakes, but in order that the great and glorious day of our parents' homecoming should be yet more glorious. Finally, when my brother was nearly seven and I nearly six, the day came. I remember sitting in the bay window of the dining room of the Home, nearly bursting with excitement, watching and waiting for them to turn the corner of the drive, and when at last they appeared, we catapulted out of the house across the front lawn and straight into their arms.

This early experience has often seemed to me to

provide a picture of the anatomy of our longing for God – the longing for someone often only dimly apprehended; the deep awareness of his existence and love even though at times he seems far away; his communication through the Scriptures. (It never seemed odd to me that God should communicate his love through the written word. I had been used to love being expressed in that way from babyhood.) And then, of course, the longing for that day when having grown up into maturity in him, into the fullness of the measure of the stature of Christ, we shall at last see him face to face.

That longing is at the heart of our prayer and is what keeps us straining forward eagerly to know God more intimately, to be immersed in him more fully. We need then to explore, and come to understand, the origin and nature of our longing for God which is universal, even if it is not recognised as such.

With the help of computer technology and modern advances in gynaecology and obstetrics, we can now pinpoint with an almost 100 per cent degree of accuracy the precise stage (day, week, month) of pre-natal life at which various limbs and organs are formed and begin to function in the foetus. We know when the heart beats, at what point the circulatory system is complete, when hair and nails develop and when the foetus is covered with that greasy, protective coating called the *vernix caseosa*. We know when the senses become developed and the foetus can not only hear but memorise, can be frightened by sudden, loud sounds, distressed by the raised voices of quarrelling parents, and soothed by music.

At nine months we, ourselves, were fully formed and emerged into this world – 'formed' in the sense of having all the potential equipment necessary to live and love, achieve and be fulfilled. But, at what stage did our *longings* begin to take birth? For we were all born into this world with powerful longings and a sense of dis-ease. There is in each of us, at the core of our being, an inner ache, a burning desire that is insatiable, irrepressible and unfathomable, a sense of incompleteness. As we grow from infancy to maturity, we focus our longings in a whole variety of ways, perhaps on another person, perhaps on goals we hope to attain or possessions we seek to acquire, or personal achievements and successes on which we have set our hearts.

Whilst these are good and proper – none in themselves meet that deepest longing of the heart, which is none other than for God himself. Even in little children – closer to primal innocence and purity than adults, who have been soiled, wearied, cheated and disillusioned by life's experiences – there is this innate, albeit unconscious, longing. It may not be as Wordsworth would have it:

> Not in entire forgetfulness
> And not in utter nakedness,
> But trailing clouds of glory do we come
> From God who is our home:
> Heaven lies about us in our infancy![2]

We may be agnostic about such a claim to pre-existence prior to conception, which suggests that children enter

4

this life with dim memories of the former one. But, whether or not we agree with Wordsworth, we must surely recognise that the image of God in them and their relationship with him have not yet been marred as in an adult. God looks on each of his created beings as special, and sees that each one is good – made for friendship with himself and restless, therefore, until they find their rest in him.[3] This is why Gregory of Nyssa speaks so often of '[returning] to the grace of that image that was established in you from the beginning'. Gregory, in fact, saw it as our lifelong task to discover and recover that part of the divine image that God has chosen to reveal specifically in us,[4] and that becomes obscured by that growing orientation towards falsity that we call 'sin'.

More often than not, our longings are without clear shape or definition. Yet so urgent and persistent are they, they can at times overwhelm and almost devour us.

On 12 February 1944, thirteen-year-old Anne Frank wrote in her now widely read diary,

> Today the sun is shining, the sky is deep blue, there is a lovely breeze and I am longing – so longing – for everything. To talk, for freedom, for friends, to be alone. And I do so long . . . to cry! I feel as if I am going to burst, and I know that it would get better with crying; but I can't, I'm restless, I go from room to room, breathe through the crack of a closed window, feel my heart beating, as if it was saying, 'Can't you satisfy my longing at last?'
>
> I believe that it is spring within me, I feel that

spring is awakening, I feel it in my whole body and soul. It is an effort to behave normally, I feel utterly confused. I don't know what to read, what to write, what to do, I only know that I am longing.[5]

So often, like Anne Frank, we are conscious of strong, consuming longings which we can neither identify nor name and which leave us confused.

The strange restlessness, the ache at the centre of our being and our inability to settle leave us dissatisfied and yet, curiously, we would not be without them. We are conscious that our longings bring us into touch with reality, make us feel more alive and drive us in a kind of spiritual wanderlust to push beyond our present horizons in a search for meaning, wholeness and completion. The search may take us down many avenues (some of them blind ones), for basically it is a form of homesickness for God who is our home, even if we are unaware of it. 'We are all making a journey home on a ticket called "longing".'[6]

I am not sure this planet is home. Do you ever have the feeling you are a tourist on earth? You'll be walking down the street and suddenly, it's like a moving postcard around you ... I'm a tourist on earth ... They have funny costumes here, but I'm fond of the place. When I remind myself I am a tourist, when I do that, I can almost recall what it's like where I come from. There's a magnet that's pulling us, pulling us against the fence of this world's limits. I have this strange feeling that I come from the other side of the fence.[7]

It would seem that Richard Bach (the creator of Jonathan Livingston Seagull) and William Wordsworth have at least some intuitions about a former existence that resonate with one another!

The limitations of success

Success appears to promise satisfaction but often fails to deliver it – for it is by nature illusory. A brilliant cellist had just given the best concert performance of her life. But backstage, to everyone's consternation, she burst into tears and wept, 'It isn't enough! It isn't enough!' She was in touch with an emptiness within that only God was big enough to fill, and that knowledge set the direction of her life. How many have been disillusioned when, having soared to successes, they have felt only a deep dissatisfaction? In terms of their need, the successes were without substance – a kind of mirage gratification ever receding into the distance, and quite unattainable.

Sometimes people regard this restlessness of spirit as a deep failure in their spiritual pilgrimage, a state of being that is opposed to a healthy journey into God. But that is to ignore the instinct in all of us to travel forward in our longings – to deeper relationships, fuller understanding, more intensive search and research into unknown territory (whether it be a field of knowledge, or exploration of the universe). Our restlessness is not born of deprivation but of experience and a longing for more of what has already begun to open up for us. We grow impatient, but know that we cannot abandon the longing, or something in us would die.

We live with this inner tension, and maturity should bring an ability to use it increasingly creatively – urging us forward without driving us. But in this world of 'instant-everything', we tend to expect instant satisfaction of our desires, instant relief of tension, instant resolution of conflicts. As Ronald Rolheiser says, 'Too much in our experience today militates against the fact that here in this life, all symphonies remain unfinished.'[8] We suffer from an addiction to 'quick fixes' which someone has dubbed 'quickaholism'.

'At the centre of our being', says Thomas Merton,

> is a point of nothingness which is untouched by sin and by illusion, a point of pure truth, a point or spark which belongs entirely to God, which is never at our disposal, from which God disposes of our lives, which is inaccessible to the fantasies of our own mind or the brutality of our own will. This little point of nothingness and *absolute poverty* is the pure glory of God in us.[9]

It is to this point that we are drawn, as surely as the tiny newborn kangaroo will grope unerringly in the darkness of its mother's pouch towards the source of sustenance. We too in the darkness of unknowing seek to drink very directly from God's life.

The furnace of the heart, the locus of our true self and

seat of our purest love, that little point of nothingness to which Merton refers, can be the crucible in which the raw minerals of our desires are purified. Without it, and frequent recourse to it, our longings could tear us apart and destroy all inner peace. How then do we live with this uncomfortable gift?

If we are serious about our journey into the heart of that furnace, a furnace of love, which is God's fire in us, and in which ultimately we shall, as the hymn says 'Behold, O Jesus, what Thou art',[10] then increasingly we have to learn to welcome our restlessness, our yearning after something or Someone greater than ourselves. We could just slide into a degenerative trivialisation of our longings, directing them towards the goal of a good life with all the social and material benefits one could wish for, hoping that all the amusements and distractions of a 'candy floss' life would somehow be enough. We have, too, to transcend that, sometimes powerful, inward desire in all of us for self-expression, for leaving an indelible impression upon our world of our uniqueness, specialness and significance which is often thwarted by the fact that others may well see us as rather ordinary, unimportant, unexciting, mediocre characters. They too are wanting to make their mark and cannot happily tolerate any rivals, or the reminder that they are, 'one among billions of others, clawing and scratching for a little uniqueness, meaning and immortality'.[11]

It is only as we recognise, and remain *peacefully* with the recognition, that it is *God* who implants our longings in the first place and draws us by them to himself, *God* who is the spark who fires our inner furnace, God alone who will in the end be our total satisfaction, God himself who gives us significance and worth, making us unique, 'precious, honoured in his eyes – and loved' – when we can grasp all that, then our longings become the absolute bedrock of our spirituality and we begin to see them as God's lure in us – 'a congenital and holy restlessness'.[12]

Longing is a hunger and a thirst

For the religious person, life is essentially a journey in which one sets out to quench a thirst, not simply to know that a God exists but to drink directly from God's own life to which man is bonded (re-ligio) in the depths of his being. Religion is thus the intuitively known and symbolically expressed desire to become who we are in God. The fulfilling of this desire is the realisation of the true self.[13]

Arriving in Botswana towards the end of six years of drought (which would continue for a seventh) gave me far clearer insight into the imagery used by biblical writers, and particularly the Psalmists, when speaking of the nature of longing – imagery which has to do with hunger, thirst and deserts.

As the deer pants for water, so my soul longs after you . . . (adapted from Psalm 42:1)

O God, you are my God, I seek you, my soul thirsts

for you; my flesh faints for you, as in a dry and barren land where there is no water. (Psalm 63:1)

During that drought, the cattle (one of Botswana's biggest resources) wandered the barren land searching for the odd blade of grass, a weed, a leaf, indeed *anything* edible – their entire skeletons visible through the skin that hung loosely on their bones. A cow, driven mad by thirst and hunger, staggered into the centre of Gaborone, with its teeming traffic and hurrying crowds, and collapsed outside a hotel. Local people rushed to find fodder of some sort, even tearing up plants from their gardens, gave it water and it revived. Other creatures were not so fortunate. Where veterinary fences had been installed, stretching for miles across vast tracts of land, to limit the movements of herds and thus contain any prevalent disease, countless animals, driven crazy by the sight of the water they could not reach, died, trapped in the wires, garrotted and left choking to death. The carnage was pitiful, the suffering horrendous. Others collapsed as they waited in broiling heat, hoping that there would be some way by which they would be able to get through to that life-saving water. They died one of the most terrible deaths imaginable – that of thirst.

People in the interior of the Kalahari desert received meagre famine-relief rations – but, even so, many still died of starvation, or lack of water.

The Psalmists were writing against that kind of background – of desert, drought and famine. That is the context we need to understand if we are to appreciate the significance and urgency of what they are saying about longing – and indeed, what Jesus was saying when he spoke of the blessedness reserved for those who 'hunger and thirst for righteousness' (Matthew 5:6). His hearers would have understood his reference with the full force of experience, for Josephus has recorded no less than ten famines in Israel between the years 169 BC and AD 70. It was not just vague pangs of hunger, the rumblings of a rebellious, spoilt-child of a stomach that Jesus had in mind, nor the longing for a genteel cup of tea (with which we are so familiar). He was referring to the hunger of starving people, and the thirst that leads to fatal dehydration. The Psalmist also paints a very telling picture of pilgrims, travelling the King's Highway en route for Jerusalem and a feast, having to pass through the valley of Baca (Psalm 84:6). For them 'dying of thirst' was not just a colloquialism, but a haunting possibility. Some seasoned travellers knew where to search in the cracked earth for hidden springs yielding a muddy ooze which nevertheless saved their lives. They were the ones who could use the dread valley as a well, and continue on their way 'singing the songs of Zion' (cf. Psalm 84:7).

Deep is the joy, then, said Jesus, of those who hunger and thirst for God, his righteousness and his Kingdom, with the intensity and all-consuming desire of desert dwellers (human and animal) in drought, and thirsty travellers passing through dried up pans and river beds.

'Burning heat' and 'furnace' are two desert-like metaphors that describe the same intensity of longing, but we need always to be mindful that it is not purely personal. There is, inextricably woven within it, a longing for God's Kingdom and its righteousness.

'When shall I come to see your face?' was a cry uttered many times by biblical writers. Maybe it seems foolish when they knew that Moses had so clearly been denied that grace. When he requested to see the face of God, he was vouchsafed only a sight of his 'back' as 'the Lord passed before him'! It was not simply that 'no man can look upon the face of God and live', but rather that a premature vision of his face would not in itself be life-giving. It would put an end to longing, striving, yearning, seeking after God, following after him in discipleship, striding to catch up with such a 'fast God' as R. S. Thomas calls him. So their request would be answered only as they watched and waited, looked and longed, to see him working hiddenly in their society and in the lives of individuals. The corollary, 'Hide not your face from me', was nearly always uttered as a lament in the face of injustice or oppression.

There will be days when we, too, will burst forth with the cry of longing, 'When shall I come to see your face?' But we must realise that the answer to it will be as we seek his face, and find it, now – in fragmentary glimpses of the divine, in broken, albeit distorted, images which nevertheless yield a fleeting vision of truth, in earthly systems, in establishing justice, truth and reconciliation on earth, in righteousness and a cleansing of society, in reverence for life in all its forms, in love expressed in anger and compassion, judgement and mercy, action and sacrifice. But we will only be able to see his face in others, in history, society and circumstances if we have lingered long in prayer with a gaze of love.[14] Our passionate longing to 'see the face of God', to know him more intimately, must needs be yoked to the prayer, 'Your Kingdom come; your will be done on earth as it is in heaven'. The genuineness of the longing can be judged by our will to actualise the Kingdom in our midst.

Moses, and many after him, discovered that the unsatisfied longing for God is what draws human beings on and propels them forward, above all else. Perhaps no thinker has realised this so passionately as Augustine. 'Longing', he observes, 'is the heart's treasury.' For the Christian this means pushing our longings to the limits. Elsewhere he put it:

> The whole life of the good Christian is a holy longing. What you desire ardently, as yet you do not see . . . by withholding of the vision, God extends the longing; through longing he extends the soul, by extending it, he makes room in it . . . So . . . let us long because we are to be filled . . . That is our life, to be exercised by longing.[15]

The following sad words were found on the desk of the avowed atheist, Bertrand Russell, after his death. But we trust that by then he had been granted what he so longed for.

At the centre of me is always and eternally a terrible

pain, a curious, wild pain, a searching for something transfigured and infinite, the Beatific Vision, God. I do not find it. I do not think it is to be found, but the love of it is my life.[16]

The prayer of yearning

Yearning may, at times, be our only prayer, though in our anxiety to 'achieve', even in prayer, we may take refuge in what seem safer aspects of it, those with more form and substance, over which we can have a degree of control – such as intercession or petition. But to flee the insecurity of unbounded yearning is to pass up the moment of grace. It is to ignore the truth that at the core of our existence, 'a transcendental neediness holds sway' which gives impetus to all our longings and desires, 'works itself out through them but is never exhausted in them'.[17]

As we simply stay with the yearning, we step over the threshold into true prayer for which much else that we have called prayer has been but preparation. That is not to undervalue it – the preparation is vital, even to the practicalities such as preparing the atmosphere and 'composition of place' (a particular place which, as we return to it, always has for us associations of prayer and which helps to rein in our scattered thoughts). We are all such fragmented beings, we need to be 'localised' when we come to pray. Worthwhile, too, is the memo pad to note down the extraneous things that intrude into our silence, and to preserve those which are promptings of the Holy Spirit, and must later be translated into action. All of that, and a gentle unwinding, enable us to breathe in the pure air of God's presence around us and in us, deepening our faith and intensifying our yearning. When we have let the muddied waters of our mind settle, plunged below the surface distractions, and gathered all our disparate energies into one still point of concentration, we are then drawn more profoundly and painfully into the furnace of our own hearts, which we experience both as a desperate inner ache and an emptiness but also paradoxically as a touch of God himself and a rich grace.

' "Heart" is often used as a metaphor to stand for the neglected faculty in many of us where discursive reason has been allowed to overshadow, and even overrule, the "intuitive, symbolic, feeling ways of knowing". We may be familiar with such phrases as "the way the heart sees", "the eyes of the heart being enlightened" (Ephesians 1:18), "it is with the heart that we see the Unseen Real", "the way the deep heart knows" (meaning the more "unconscious" reaches of our being)',[18] and they are all expressions of a need to give due weight to that faith which is not in conflict with reason but can go far beyond it. 'The rational faculty has all too often been elevated whilst the intuitive, feeling mind has been denied or even denigrated.'

The Bible, however, knows nothing of such a false dichotomy, which sets discursive, rational thinking over against the intuitive-feeling mind. 'In biblical language, the heart is the centre of the human spirit, from which spring emotions, thought, motivations, courage and action – indeed "the well-spring of life".'

The 'heart' represents head knowledge as well as heart knowledge – there is no need for them to be in collision – and 'instead of speaking of healing the rift between the two, the Bible talks quite simply of *cleansing the heart* – a cleansing which starts the very radical process of transformation in every faculty, preparing the whole person for a *transposition* – an infilling of God's Spirit'.

As we penetrate the furnace of the heart and know ourselves 'on fire' with longing, we experience something of what St Paul meant when he spoke of 'straining forward' in an *epektasis*[19] of love-longing – straining forward eagerly after God as an athlete does to breast the tape first at the finishing line; as a dog does when it strains at the leash longing to be set free to enjoy an energetic, unfettered run. They are good images for they speak of being 'pointed' in one direction, single-minded, unswerving in intent, and totally focused. Gregory of Nyssa's most significant contribution to Christian thought was (and is) his view of the Christian life as one of unceasing advance, 'straining forward to what lies ahead'. What matters, he claims, is 'the *epektasis* of love and longing, permeating the whole of life'.[20] Yet this yearning, though never satisfied, 'is . . . that eternal, inexplicable longing that knows no dissatisfaction and want'.[21]

Conflict of desire

Some years ago, the BBC asked some Sisters of our Community to take part in a programme on 'Stress'. Quite why *we* were chosen was not clear – but we acceded to the request. What emerged, in the discussions during the series, was the place and force that conflicting desires (as well as conflicting demands) have in the whole area of stress. Since we are all such complex beings, none of us escapes this conflict entirely. We are always yearning for someone or something – either that we have not yet met or experienced, or having done so, find ourselves longing for more. The natural way of dealing with this yearning (for we also fear it) is to escape into compulsive activity, 'a chasing after the wind', to avoid silence and solitude lest they make us face unwelcome changes which they are likely to bring about in us. For our 'staying with' the prayer of yearning is not a vague form of 'devotional mooning', it is the opening of ourselves to radical, inner transformation which one day, by God's grace, will be total.

For this we require not only inner and outer stillness, but a quite deliberate act of will in which we seek to set aside conflicting desires and dreams. We are not out 'to go places' in prayer. It is far more necessary to stop and strip away the desires that have become idolatrous accretions which hinder and block our growth. For the more we turn to false gods to satisfy our hunger, the more starved and shrivelled we become spiritually.

One day the Teacher said, 'It is much easier to travel than to stop.'

'Why?' the disciples demanded to know.

'Because', the Teacher said, 'as long as you travel to a goal, you can hold on to a dream. When you stop, you must face reality.'

'But how shall we ever change if we have no goals or dreams?' the disciples asked.

'Change that is real', said the Teacher, 'is change that is not willed. Face reality and unwilled change will happen.'[22]

Simplicity of desire

The journey from complexity of desire to simplicity is a long and arduous one. But some have shown us that it is possible. Richard Rolle could say, 'All my desires are one desire, and that for nought but Thee.'[23] And the Psalmist was able to write: 'One thing have I desired of the Lord, that will I seek after' (Psalm 27:4, italics mine). What an enviable position to be in! To have such unity of desire is, as T. S. Eliot has said, 'a condition of complete simplicity, costing not less than everything'. Whereas, for most of us, even our purest desires are multi-faced, tinged with some ulterior motive, or a touch of self-seeking, and there is much sifting, sorting and weeding to be done.

The literal meaning of simplicity is 'one pleat' – a powerful image as we imagine all desires, pruned of idolatry, being folded into one large pleat, and thus embraced by and enfolded into God.

Someone has spoken of the 'expulsive power of a great longing'. As we live honestly into our heart's longings, we find we can deal with those which are superficial or unworthy – and expel, convert or deepen them. If our chief desire is for God, other desires will either be absorbed and sanctified by it or banished. 'If your eye is single,' said Jesus, 'your whole body will be full of light,' (Matthew 6:22). ('Single' means single-minded: 'the intention of our spirit directed to God himself alone', as the writer of The Cloud of Unknowing puts it.) The part becomes redemptive of the whole. God who is the source and end of our desiring is able to encompass even some of our lesser desires and simplify them into a unity – if we consent to his purifying work. For, from now on,

> your whole life . . . must be one of longing, if you are to achieve perfection. And this longing must be in the depths of your will, put there by God, with your consent. But a word of warning: he is a jealous lover and will brook no rival; he will not work in your will if he has not sole charge. His will is that you should look at him and let him have his way. You must, however, guard your spiritual windows and doorways against enemy attacks.[24]

That guarding of the heart is vital, as the Book of Proverbs tells us, 'Above all else, guard your heart for it is the well spring of life', (Proverbs 4:23). Simplicity goes hand in hand with vigilance, with the resolute rejection of the temptation to open ourselves to what cannot be folded into one pleat of desire. There are choices to be made. We need not be at the mercy of our changing desires and the siren voices of seduction that would draw us away from our longing for and contemplation of God. Since an intimate knowledge of God grows only in peace, the Evil One puts disturbance at the heart of his strategy. He attempts to 'lead us out on to the field of imagination or false lights' where we come under fierce attack. Rather than trying by ourselves to ward off imaginations, reasonings and desires that trouble us, which is exactly what he would like, we need in faith to take refuge in the fact that he cannot

> act directly on our wills. He *can*, however, make use of our feelings – either by instilling anxiety into them, or by pushing them to extremes and to a violence they do not naturally have. Whereas the Holy Spirit acts in the depths of our soul by love, the devil acts on our feelings by creating disturbance.[25]

But as Isaiah put it: 'You will keep in perfect peace the one whose mind is stayed on you, because he trusts in you' (Isaiah 26:3). A more recent hymn writer has expressed it, 'You alone are my heart's desire, and I long to worship you.' Or as the Psalmist said, 'You, O Lord, are the thing (One) that I long for' (Psalm 71:4a, Coverdale version).

Single-mindedness, singleness of heart are of the

essence of simplicity and need a constant guarding of
the heart if we are to be saved from duplicity. They will
unify our desires until the whole of our life is governed
by one burning passion and our prayer becomes wholly
dependent on 'the fidelity of our longing'.[26] For as the
author of *The Cloud of Unknowing* has written, once desire
for God is unleashed we must 'stand in desire' all the
rest of our lives![27]

> O you, who have come into the depth of my heart,
> enable me to concentrate solely
> on this depth of my heart!

> O you, who are guest in the depth of my heart,
> enable me also to penetrate
> into this depth of my heart!

> O you, who are at home in the depth of my heart,
> enable me to sit peacefully
> in this depth of my heart!

> O you, who alone belong in the depth of my heart,
> enable me to dive deep and lose myself
> in this depth of my heart!

> O you, who are quite alone in the depth of my
>   heart,
> enable me to disappear into you
> in the depth of my heart![28]

TWO

WEBS OF ILLUSION
The Sifting of Longings

*Let us spread our desires as if they were cloaks for Christ's passing
so that by means of our aspirations, he can enter our heart,
ensconce himself completely in us, transform us totally in him
and express himself entirely in us.*

Andrew of Crete

*A life based on desires is like a spider's web. Woven about us by
the Father of lies (the Devil) — the Enemy of our Soul — it is a
frail tissue of vanities without substance, and yet it can catch us
and hold us fast, delivering us up to him as a prisoner. Nevertheless,
the illusion is only an illusion — nothing more. It should be as
easy for us to break through this tissue of lies as it is for us to
destroy a spider's web with a movement of the hand.*

Gregory of Nyssa

The more honest we are in sifting our authentic desires
from the inauthentic, for true desire and intensity of
feeling are not necessarily the same thing, the more we
will discover who we truly are. Our loves shape and
define us. This requires some hard and painful work of
discernment since we are all incredibly practised in self-
deception. We need to 'surf the web' of our multifarious
desires – to probe their real nature, identify those that

23

are trivial and relatively unimportant, and engage with those that stem from the deeper levels of our beings.

Gregory of Nyssa was clearly thinking of the first of these – the trinkets of this world that can capture and hold us, the illusory achievements. He says:

> The pursuit in this life of things like honour, reputation, dignities, glory, fortune: all these are the work of life's spiders . . . But those who rise to the heights, escape, with a flick of the wing, from the spiders of this world.
>
> Only those, who like flies, are heavy and without energy remain caught in the glue of this world and are taken and bound, as though in nets, by honours, pleasures, praise and manifold desires, and thus become the prey of the beast that seeks to capture them.[1]

To sweep away the cobwebs once is not enough, of course. We don't bind ourselves to worldly attachments simply by one wrong choice, but by many.

> A person can spin a whole net of falsities around his spirit [says Gregory] by the repeated consecration of the whole self to values that do not exist. He [she] exhausts him [her] self in the pursuit of mirages that ever fade, and are renewed as fast as they have faded, drawing him [her] further and further into the wilderness where he [she] must die of thirst.[2]

Gregory wrote this in his homily on Ecclesiastes. He reckoned that the 'vanity of vanities' which so exercised the Preacher is a life not merely of deluded thoughts and aspirations, but above all, a life of 'ceaseless, sterile activity'. What is more, in such a life, the very intensity of the activity itself is a clue to the measure of illusion.

The obsessive preoccupation with the trinkets this world has to offer he likens to children playing on the sand. Their delight is in the actual activity of playing. When they have finished building, their pleasure ends – they know that once they have stopped building, it will all fall down – nothing will be left but a heap of sand. (An interesting insight into child's play in the fourth century!)

Compulsive activity is one way of staving off the pain of unfulfilled desires, of relegating them to oblivion and keeping the spirit numb. But it brings only temporary relief. It acts merely as a brand of emotional pain-killer.

If we do not seek the desert of solitude and silence, however much we may fear it, and face our illusions head on, we condemn ourselves to a far more deadly and insidious wilderness where we live hopelessly entangled in a web of illusions. We are all driven by the Spirit at times into the desert of solitude and silence, as Jesus was, to wrestle with our illusions. For part of our growth in the spiritual life involves a necessary disillusionment.

Thomas Merton and Gregory echo one another, in that Merton once said:

The earthly desires people cherish are shadows. There is no true happiness in fulfilling them. Why then do we pursue joys without substance? Because the pursuit itself has become the substitute for joy. Unable to rest in anything we achieve, we determine to forget our discontent in a ceaseless quest for new satisfactions. In this pursuit, desire itself becomes our chief satisfaction. The goods that so disappoint us when they are within our grasp can stimulate our interest when they elude us in the present or past.

These are the real distractions (not so much the unbidden thoughts and images that float across the screen of our mind when we try to pray).

'Distraction,' observes Pascal, 'is the only thing that seems to bring us consolation and yet is itself our greatest desolation' – because it diverts us from the one thing that can help us in our ascent to truth. That 'one thing' is the sense of our emptiness, our poverty, our limitations, and of the inability of worldly values to satisfy our profound need for reality and truth. We cannot find true happiness unless we deprive ourselves of the ersatz happiness of empty diversion.[3]

Longings versus cravings

How then can we best discern whether we are clinging to illusions or deepening in authentic desire?

True desire is accompanied by an inner quickening, even whilst leaving us unsatisfied. It has within it a creative force. Therein lies the difference. True desire leaves us *unsatisfied* – always longing for more. Illusion leaves us *dis-satisfied* – with a sour after-taste of having been cheated. What we long for is always just out of reach. And yet, in our fearfulness, we surf only the mere fringes of our desires rather than aiming for the centre, that point of nothingness, our essential space and emptiness, where the furnace of the heart ever blazes, and where our true longing is constantly being kept alive and refined.

We are on dangerous ground if we heed our infinite desires without question and allow them to seduce us. For the desire that is alone life-giving is our ever deepening longing for God. When we exchange that for the deadening effect of illusory desires, or even admissible but more superficial desires, there is an inner sense of loss, of having missed the pearl of great price. We may hold other perfectly good and proper pearls in our hands, but we are still restless and discontented.

So, it is an essential task, this discerning of false or transitory desires of the heart, for we all have cravings that lead to addictive tendencies. Each of us is given to some form of idolatry. 'Addiction means being so completely possessed that one is enslaved, deprived of inner freedom and ultimately of personal integrity. It is the ghastly process of "losing one's soul" '.[4] This is why it is so important to spend time reflecting on our longings and their true nature, for even though we may not be addicted to a form of substance abuse – a physical dependence on anything that will induce a mood change, such as drugs, alcohol, caffeine, or even chocolate – we may well be hooked on work, sport, sex, food, gambling, TV soaps, computer games, on-line chats, or even religious activities, all of which fill a big gap in our lives and point to deeper emotional needs. Each of them in some way or other leads us to compulsive behaviour, loss of freedom and personal deterioration. And, of course, the very fact that addiction – to anything – gets a stronger and stronger hold on us, only results in an ever-*increasing* dependency. Perhaps one of the most powerful, common and insidious of addictions, in our time, is that of making money. So much energy, preoccupation and concern are invested in that servitude of Mammon, in that idol called 'Materialism'. But as Selwyn Hughes has pointed out, this is no new thing. What Jesus spoke of most often was not prayer, or love or forgiveness. It was money – the love of it, the dependence on it, the making of it by fair means or foul, the extortion, usury, bribery and betrayal to which it led, the sitting loose to it so that our treasure is not that which is transitory, rapidly suffering corruption or devaluation, but is lasting and focused on things eternal. That in itself is significant, and his warning that money can be the biggest potential idol in our lives is as true today as it was in his.

These forms of addiction need more than Gregory's flick of the wing to remove the spiders' webs. They require keys to liberate people from their prison bars.

James Houston very helpfully suggests three areas of addiction which may need to be confronted.[5] Firstly, *personal addiction*, which requires that I take far more responsibility for myself as a person in my own right, with greater moral choices than I may have realised. I *am* free to stand out against the crowd, to refuse to submit to the 'herd mentality' – free to act with personal autonomy and integrity. 'How many teenagers fall into addictive traps, because of their over-riding need to gain social approval?' Whether it be drinking, smoking, drug-taking, glue-sniffing, joy-riding or pre-marital sex – it is all too easy to fall prey to the expectations and acceptable norms of contemporary society, and especially one's peer group. 'Everyone is doing it' becomes sufficient justification.

Secondly, confronting *family addiction* means recognising patterns of hidden, abnormal behaviour, 'conspiracies' that have been perpetuated and perceived as 'normal' in family life. It may take a real rebel to recognise what is wrong and to break the chain of, e.g., mental, psychological or physical abuse, 'clannish' and exclusive behaviour, or other deep-rooted, oppressive and even pathological forms of behaviour.

Thirdly, confronting *societal addiction* means pinpointing and combatting widespread abuse of one sort or another 'within the previously unexamined or unjudged standards of society . . . There is a certain social hypocrisy that focuses on the "drug problem" while ignoring many other kinds of addictions'[6] that our society not only tolerates but actually encourages – widescale corporate greed leading to vast economic gaps in society and trade monopolies; 'addictions such as workaholism,

professionalism, perfectionism, consumerism, porno-
graphy, sexism, and many more'.[7]

Whilst we can be greatly indebted to James Houston
for identifying these three areas of addiction, I would
want to add a further one, *institutional addiction*, in which
people become prisoners to routine. In any institution,
it becomes wearing and time-consuming to be without
proper routines or to have the normal ones disrupted
too often – whether it be those of a school, a hospital,
a church, a religious community, or simply a family. But
when we are in absolute bondage to routine, when
commendable orderliness and necessary structures take
on the form of sacred rituals from which there can be
no deviation, no matter how much a situation cries out
for flexibility, no matter how lost in antiquity the
reason for doing things in a certain way has become;
when our security is dependent on sticking slavishly
to the conventions; when the level of our happiness
corresponds exactly to the degree of our resistance to
change – then we are helplessly addicted. A certain
amount of conditioning can be helpful – and we are
conditioned to some extent by our upbringing, culture
and community – it saves us having to make countless
small choices every day about relatively unimportant
things. But conditioning itself can become addictive, if
we are not aware of what is going on.

If Jesus were incarnate again, I could imagine him
saying: 'The Son of Man is Lord of routine, and not the
other way round!' The systems are there to serve us, not
we the systems. But how many of us, particularly those

of us who live in large institutions with long histories and strong traditions, are actually in sin in this respect? How far have we bowed the knee to the idol called 'Routine'? How far have our routines become 'habits to hide behind', as Gerald May suggests?[8] Have remarks such as: 'It is our custom' or, 'But we've always done it like this' (which someone has called rather wryly 'The Seven Last Words of the Church'), been allowed to be the final word when any possibility of change arises?

It may not be a form of addiction that causes headaches to the Security Police or Drug Squads, but nevertheless we have a problem, and a major one at that. For in our addiction we cannot be open to the fresh springs that the Holy Spirit is always causing to bubble up to enliven us. Our closed minds and robotic patterns of behaviour have made us subhuman.

Some forms of addiction can quite certainly be labelled as sinful. But other forms are not so readily identifiable. Perfectly harmless pursuits, if they get a hold on us and leave us unfree, take on the characteristics of addiction. I recall as a student becoming so 'hooked' on chess that I cut lectures, was completely distracted in prayer, and even during sermons (which I normally love) was busy working out the next moves in a game. It had to go – but there's nothing wrong with chess, in itself. It's a fine game, highly to be recommended. In our technological age, computer games are a raging obsession with young children and adults alike. Others are hooked on videos (particularly violent ones), rubbishy novels, TV, the pursuit of the body beautiful, and even housework – for there are many sacred ways in a kitchen! Anything that absorbs an inordinate amount of time and energy has the potential for becoming an addiction.

It is essential, therefore, to examine our compulsions and recognise where they are coming from. How far might we have abdicated our personal freedom? We need to reflect on the things that hold and bind us. Do we possess our possessions or do they possess us? What about our chronic negativity? Where do our feelings of inadequacy stem from? What of our compulsive need to make a good impression, to be well thought of – so deeply rooted in us that we can't cope with any criticism, and become judgemental of others, boosting our egos by 'running them down'? We may develop a tendency to control or dominate others, to exaggerate and dramatise things in order to give ourselves a sense of importance, to assume omniscience on every subject, in every situation. What of our perpetual feeling of lostness, as though something vital is missing from our lives, which leaves us whining and complaining and for ever descending into the 'poor-little-me' spiral? What of our neurotic defensiveness, our predisposition to moodiness?

Addiction to success and efficiency

Of course the addiction which afflicts countless numbers of people, in every walk of life, is the need to succeed. It's not altogether surprising given that our whole educational system is geared to achievement and success.

During a visit to South Africa in 1993, I used regularly to pass a nursery school, on the front walls of which were painted in very large letters, 'LITTLE ACHIEVERS'. It appalled me that even the name of the school could imply a terrible pressure placed upon children of such a tender age! For, after all, how does one measure achievement or success? The 'League Tables' now published by the British government give satisfaction to top-scoring schools in public exams. But what about the school in a down-town deprived area where they have been able to eliminate much of the bullying, create a little colour, fun and beauty for children who have precious little of any in their homes? What of the dyslexic or hard-of-hearing child who has made huge strides in transcending his/her handicap? Fortunately many schools now reward such achievements at their annual prizegiving ceremonies. But it's academic and sporting successes that still seem to get the spotlight and public acclaim. One recent commercial showed a scene from a football match, and the caption that passed across the screen read: 'It's not a game. It's a sport. It's about being first.' 'Winning is not everything, it is the only thing!' This is not just cheerleaders' rhetoric. It says a great deal about the attitude being instilled into young people today, an attitude that led one very bright 15-year-old to commit suicide. After getting straight 'A's in all her term and exam work, she dropped on one paper to a 'B'. Her parents' disappointment was so keen, their silence so pregnant with icy disapproval, she simply couldn't stand it. For once she had come second instead of first, and it was tantamount to failure. 'If I fail in what I do, then I fail in what I am,' she wrote on her suicide note.[9]

Ambition is seen as a commendable driving force. The following comment was written by his housemaster on the final report of a boy leaving one of Britain's top public schools. 'This boy has no desire to be rich or famous. What's wrong with him?' – which actually says more about the master and the system than about the boy himself.

The success syndrome also haunts the Church in all sorts of insidious ways. At clergy gatherings, I have sometimes joined a group chatting together over tea, and, almost invariably, the conversation has been about the number of new families that have joined the church, the attendances at services, the number of baptisms, confirmations, marriages, etc., the amount raised at the church fete, and the structural improvements and repairs they have been able to undertake. Often there is a genuine motive to succeed for the sake of the Gospel, a desire that the organisation of the church should be efficient, vigorous and God-honouring. Certainly energetic church life, with a thriving outreach programme and a deeply caring, committed fellowship is good and makes a powerful impact upon a local community – where a sleepy church drifting along cuts no ice. To be ambitious for the Church of Jesus Christ is fine provided we remind ourselves constantly that it is his Church, his values and understanding of success, his name which must be honoured, and we are not driven by a frenetic need simply to appear successful and acquire a wide and flattering reputation. In such conversation groups, I have noticed the sad, silent clergy who feel they have no success stories to relate.

But in the reckoning of Jesus, the numbers in a congregation may fall away simply *because* the minister is succeeding in leading people deeper and deeper into a vital relationship with God, leading them to the heart of faith and commitment – which may involve saying the unpopular word. But it is exactly what he himself did. When 'others went no more with him' because they couldn't take what he was saying, he turned to his disciples and said, 'Will you also go away?' And Peter replied, 'Lord, to whom can we go? You have the words of eternal life' (John 6:68). *That* was success. Fewer followers, but one who was moving closer to the centre of truth.

Missionaries, too, were apt, in days gone by, to tell only their success stories as they toured the churches on deputation. They described the dramatic conversions and healings, the successes of building schools and hospitals, the pioneering ventures and the encouraging responses to their preaching. It was, of course, what the churches wanted to hear. But I once decided to tell the other side of the story. I spoke of the humiliation and frustration of initially not being able to speak the language, of having to go back to the baby-stage of learning how to talk all over again and making the most awful 'howlers' into the bargain. I spoke of the loneliness, the homesickness, the lack of appreciative eyes, encouraging voices and an applauding public. For so often there wasn't anything to applaud or write home about. It was all very humdrum and ordinary work, only made unusual, and sometimes unusually difficult, by virtue of being in a different climate and culture. Success in those circumstances could only be thought of in terms of faithfully going on going on. Most disturbing of all, to the congregation I was addressing, were my references to the failures of missionaries in relationships – the breakdowns in charity, the personality clashes, the refusals to be reconciled, the disunity and rows – often exacerbated by the toll taken by heat and an inadequate diet.

How could I say that the outward successes – the excellent exam results, the very encouraging reports following an inspection of schools and colleges, the incredible feat of an unskilled missionary in building an auditorium to seat 2,000 – were actually very secondary to the 'success' of God's grace in bringing two missionaries, involved in a long-standing dispute, to the point where they could meet in chapel early each morning to pray?

How do we measure success? At an Oxford University Mission, Jean Vanier gave us a powerful parable of success. He told us of an Olympic Games for mentally and physically handicapped people. Andrew (one of the L'Arche competitors) was an extremely fast sprinter who stood an excellent chance of winning the 100 metres final. He trained daily and enthusiastically, for he had set his heart on a gold medal. The day came. Andrew was in top form and everyone was confident that he would succeed in getting his heart's desire. Only one other competitor, George, posed any real threat to him. So any victory would not simply be a walkover. The race began and Andrew and George were out ahead – Andrew drawing further away and gradually closing in on his longed for prize. Then George stumbled and fell. Andrew stopped in his tracks, ran back to George, helped him up, and hand in hand, they ran together to the finishing tape.

If only we could learn the meaning of success from Andrew. 'We value our degrees and our titles, and fail to learn the wisdom of the simple or the scope of our deficiencies,' says Joan Puls.[10]

If only the world could receive the wisdom enshrined in *that* success story – that giving one another a helping hand, joining forces in an enterprise, cancelling the Third World debt, is a far greater mark of true success, than trampling over one another ruthlessly in order to be first, top, and the greatest achiever.

It is impossible to have genuine, uninhibited relationships with one another if every achievement is a cause for jealousy, resentment and an overly competitive spirit. Jealousy will always stalk us if our sense of worth and self-image must constantly be inflated by our successes. We will be thrown into misery over and over again if we fail to achieve, fail to stand out as special, fail to take the centre stage and shine as a star – when we secretly envy and hate those more talented than we are; when we are for ever sizing ourselves up against others and making comparisons.

The enigma separating us from each other becomes ever more difficult to penetrate as we become more and more obsessed with ourselves and our need to be special, to sit above. We live in jealousy, competition and violence. The other is perennially perceived as a threat.

We need to let the mind and heart of Christ exorcise this demon from our lives. In the mind and heart of Christ . . . the other's special talents are not seen as a threat but as something which enhances all of life, our life included.[11]

This is true for nations as well as individuals. If, as individuals, we accepted this there would be a lot less jealousy, competition and violence. If as nations we accepted it, we would not be poised on the brink of nuclear and economic destruction.

If we have any problem in identifying our addictive tendencies, the people most able to help us are, of course, those with whom we live and work. It will almost certainly be painful but better that than to reach a point where our addiction to a substance or a process, to routine, success, efficiency, increases to such an extent that we become more and more detached from reality, whilst our self-esteem correspondingly withers to puny micro-size. Once we have turned from our dependence and idolatry in a true *metanoia*,[12] we need to be extra vigilant lest we get sucked into the seductive pathways that will take us straight back into bondage. 'It is one and the same thing to be "Holy" and to be

38

"free". Sin is everything which entails a loss of freedom.'[13]

The human heart's desire for love

There is in each of us a deep and right yearning for love – we all came into the world with it, trustfully expecting the yearning to be fulfilled as part of our birthright. Some have been fortunate to have this expectation met as near perfectly as is possible for imperfect human beings. They have been enveloped all their lives in a sense of security and healthy self-esteem. For others, the need was hardly recognised, and in others still, tragically denied. But when love is not met, it leaves people unfulfilled and longing for completeness. Even rich adult friendships and a loving marriage will not entirely compensate for the lack of a secure childhood foundation – of knowing one was loved, wanted, the source of great pride and joy. It is the unmet longing for love which is at the root of much compulsive behaviour – behaviour such as kleptomania (a compulsive tendency to theft for its own sake), or an obsessive need to cram one's diary with social engagements to avoid encountering any spaces in life, or compulsive spending sprees. It is an attempt to fill an emptiness. The very fact that stuffing oneself with whatever – food, novels or trashy magazines, even knowledge – does nothing to fill the fathomless void turns the compulsion into an addiction. Some seek consolation not so much in bodily in-filling but in emotional satisfaction – ever craving attention, approval, a means of inflating self-importance, and creating all manner of dependence.

No amount of human love, however, will ever eliminate the sense of incompleteness that we all feel tugging at us in our depths. For that longing for completion is the soul searching for God. Our restless hearts will only find rest in him, as Augustine said, because we were made for union with him.

And yet, that sense of incompleteness has always been disastrously misunderstood by so many throughout the ages. In their desperate hunger for a completeness we can never fully attain in this life, people have been compelled to resort to all manner of idols. Today's idols that claim so much devotion and energy bear such titles as money, sex, power and, indeed, every conceivable form of pleasure. The chief end of humankind, far from 'glorifying God and enjoying him for ever', is to indulge in what is thought of as the 'good life' (largely influenced by commercial advertising or 'soaps'), a life of wealth, luxury of every kind, beauty, physical prowess, rapid ascent up the promotional ladder, and the ability to be endlessly manipulative (which accounts for the extraordinary popularity of a programme like *Dallas*). There is little distinction between 'needs' and 'wants', and when we examine them, it comes as quite a shock to discover how very few real 'needs' we have. The common philosophy is: 'What I want, I must have – and at whatever cost.' Hence, infidelity to marriage vows (and even to the tacit commitment between live-in partners), ruthless competition, greed, corruption and domination flourish at every level.

And all of it is a fruitless search for what the 'world' can never give. For love is not about what we can get, or about being fulfilled, but about self-giving, sacrifice, 'connectedness, communion, creativity and joyful expansiveness'.[14] It is also about intimacy and vulnerability, which carry frightening risks and are far more difficult to achieve than mere sex. For Christians it is about reconciliation and forgiveness, both of which are extremely costly.

We all long for love, and yet strangely run away from it and turn to our addictions to compensate for the hole at the core of our being. 'We are afraid', writes Gerald May, 'of the agony, the uncertainty, and the terrifying space that come from refusing to act out an addiction.'[15]

> Our attachments to substances, performance and responsibility help us to mask our true desires, offer the illusion of control, and fuel the life of efficiency upon which our society is based. But while efficiency can fill our days, occupy our minds, and direct our emotions, it cannot fulfil our desire for love and communion, leaving us vulnerable to addiction.[16]

It is a myth – this expectation that we shall find complete fulfilment in this life. We shall always feel unfulfilled in some area of our life – that's quite normal. Many of us feel driven to fill up every space in our lives rather than live into our emptiness. We are actually afraid of space. Yet, why is that? Why do we run from the very thing that could heal us? Partly it is because we fear what spaciousness will reveal to us. Spaciousness gives us clarity of vision and that inevitably brings to light truths about ourselves we would rather not face. Geoffrey Moorhouse called his book recording his journey across the Sahara *The Fearful Void*. He had good reason to think of the geographical desert as a fearful void in which humans feel themselves reduced to infinitesimal dots on the horizon, vulnerable to the elements and constantly in danger of becoming lost. But it is not the grandeur and vastness of the geographical desert that constitutes the most fundamental fear. It is the journey into the interior desert which we must needs make, however frightening. Moorhouse's motive in undertaking the journey, in the first place, was equally to face his own fearful, inner void, to confront his own desert of emptiness and illusion.

In the book of Hosea, using the infidelity of Gomer and the incredible generosity of Hosea as an analogy, the Lord says that he will allure Israel and lead her into the wilderness and there woo her as in the early days of their relationship. There, in that space apart, he will speak tenderly to her again and win back her love and loyalty. He will search her out and 'redeem' her from the slavery into which she is about to be sold (Hosea 3:2).

We, too, are led into the deserts of our hearts to be redeemed and liberated from our seductive desires – to be saved. And it is interesting that in biblical Hebrew, the letters *yodh* and *shin* combine to form a root that denotes 'space and the freedom and security which is gained by the removal of constriction'. From this YS root we get the words *yesha* and *yeshua* referring to salvation.[17] It is easy to see the connection between space and salvation, for space is freedom – and in our inner desert it is freedom from oppression, domination, compulsions and drivenness that is offered us. Just as silence is the freedom *not* to have to talk, so space is the freedom *not* to have to be busy and active. 'Our passion needs elbow room.'[18] Like Israel, the desert is the place of encounter with God, as well as with our inner demons. It is the place where he woos us into a deeper love relationship with himself; where illusions, addictions and false desires are purged.

The journey requires aloneness and courage. It cannot be made by proxy. It is helped by literal, geographical space – a solitary walk, a retreat in some beautiful setting, by the stark simplicity of an uncluttered room, by time free from interruptions and demands. But chiefly it requires a willingness for 'the Encounter', for the 're-alignment of our attitudes towards spaciousness'[19] where we begin to discover it as presence rather than absence. It is the place where in true prayer we are stripped of our illusions and grow towards Reality.

Etty Hillesum speaks of the 'battlefield of our inner space'.[20] For it is not only a matter of entering the eternal space of God, but of turning one's innermost being into a 'vast empty plain – so that something of "God" can enter us, and something of Love too'.[21]

'Empty yourself and see that I am God' – *'Vacate, et videte quoniam ego sum Deus'* – is the Vulgate version of Psalm 46:10.[22]

What might the landscapes of these deserts be like?

For the hyper-active there is the desert of solitude and inactivity, where we learn the painful art of doing nothing.

For the perfectionist, there is the desert of imperfection where we learn that our compulsive need is often met at the expense of love, and lays a heavy burden on others.

The academic may need to enter a desert of solitude to discover in what ways scholarship has been allowed to substitute for warm relationships, and erudition has held people at bay.

The do-good-er will possibly have to enter the desert of powerlessness and learn how, for the sake of love and in order to respect the space, and reverence the need, for distance from another, it is necessary sometimes to be useless.

The change-resistant addict to routine may have to discover the desert as a place of flux and constantly changing landscape; a trackless waste with no fixed paths; a place where the wind of the Spirit can disturb everything and one's only safety is to be guided by the heavens.

For those who are compulsive givers but disabled receivers, there is the desert of need and inadequacy where we face the reality of our emotional deficiencies and manipulative powers.

For the status-seeker, there is the desert of ordinariness where we learn the meaning of true humility and genuine inner authority.

The quietist learns in the desert that true peace-making is not a matter of taking the line of least resistance. It is costly in the extreme and requires boldness of confrontation and holy rage.

The clown may have to enter the desert of desolation to learn that life's pain cannot for ever be repressed or masked by engineered fun and artificial enjoyment – a desert where escape is impossible and pain may, for the time being, fill the horizon.

In the history of Israel, the desert was always a great teacher. It is so for us, in numerous different contexts.

In all our discussion of the search for God, the longing after God, we must be careful not to over-emphasise the human striving as though God remains distant and unmoved. We only love him because he first loved us. He takes the initiative and runs out to meet us in all our prodigal wanderings. An experiential knowledge of being swept into a huge embrace of that infinite love rescues us from our tortured, frenzied seeking of fulfilment through our compulsions and addictions, and enables us to penetrate our deserts courageously and creatively.

Cashing in on longings

'The Lure of the Cult' was the title of an article in *Time* magazine (7 April 1997) which points to one of the biggest 'spider's webs' of our age. Appearing as it did after the mass suicide of 39 members of the Heaven's Gate Cult in Rancho Santa Fe, California, the article is a forceful reminder of the sheer strength of that inner longing that ultimately can only be met by God. Many of the cult members had church backgrounds. The cult leader, Marshall Applewhite, had been the choir director in an Anglican church. They were all 'seeking', but tragically did not find the satisfaction they were looking for in institutional Christianity. The three reporters[23] in the *Time* article claim that 'in times of upheaval and uncertainty, people seek out leaders with power and charisma' because 'the established churches are too faint-hearted to satisfy the wilder kinds of spiritual hunger'. As we approach the millennium, we are told that it is 'coaxing all the crazies out of the woodwork. They bring with them a twitchy, hybrid of spirituality and pop obsession. Part Christian, part Asian mystic, part Gnostic, part *X-Files*, it mixes immemorial longings with the latest in trivial sentiments . . . overheated computer chat and New Age vapourings.'

These 39 cult members sacrificed themselves to what writers call, 'the new millennial kitsch'. That's the cultural by-product in which 'spiritual yearnings are captured in New Age gibberish, then edged with the glamour of sci-fi and the consolations of a toddler's bed time'.

It is a strange coincidence that the Internet terminology uses words like *Website* to indicate one's place on the World Wide Web. For the Heaven's Gate group it was a web of illusion on a massive, global and dangerous scale. For the quick recruitment of new congregations, the Internet is a magical opportunity. It is persuasive, clandestine and far-reaching. For better or worse, it enables people to enter a world of unreality, where the on-line context cannot really connect with real life. 'The Internet allows different belief systems to meet and mate,' says Stephen O'Leary.[24] What you then get is this 'millennial stew'. One wonders what further fantasies and horrors will emerge before AD 2000!

It is yet to be discovered how many have been drawn into the web of Heaven's Gate philosophy by means of computer chat. But what kind of people are attracted to such a weird set of beliefs? Psychologists say that applicants require *'only an unsatisfied spiritual longing'* – (italics mine). Those longings are sufficiently urgent to drive people to submit to belief systems that are bizarre in the extreme, which in this case included the conviction that the group would be picked up by a UFO sheltering behind the comet Hale-Bopp.

So, while the Heaven's Gate cult were preparing for their quiet, meticulous and orderly extinction, five members of the Order of the Solar Temple blew themselves up (quite literally) sky high in a cottage in the French Canadian village of St Casimir, bringing the number of suicides in this cult to 74 since 1994. Eighteen years ago the world was horrified at the discovery of the 900 bodies of cult members in Jonestown, Guyana, and in 1993 came the conflagration of the Branch Davidians at Waco.

These were ordinary, normal people driven by an unmet longing. We are told that the approach of 2000 has swelled the ranks of the fearful and credulous. On the Internet, cults are multiplying in service to strange gods, and to a whole range of mythical interterrestrial creatures. Millennial fever will be on a lot of minds, says Carl Raschke, a cult specialist at the University of Denver – who predicts an explosion of more weird and bizarre cults – and many eyes will be trained on the sky, searching for portents of possible importance. For centuries the stars have been where the beliefs of religion, science and the occult have converged. It seems unbelievable that people can be so gullible – but it is happening, for their profoundest longing is starved.

'The Heaven's Gate philosophy added all its astronomical trappings to a core of weirdly adulterated Christianity.' It has taught us amongst other things that 'the religious impulse sometimes thrives on false sentiment, emotional need and cultural fluff'. The three journalists conclude that, 'In its search for meaning, the mind is apt to go down some wrong paths and to mistake its own reflection for the face of God.'

For us it is yet another appalling reminder that there are those who are desperately longing for meaning, significance and truth, and cannot somehow find or encounter them in Christ's body, the Church, in the One who alone can meet that longing. Their despair seems not to have been recognised for what it was – and that is a serious judgement upon a church that has been enfeebled by self-concern. For them, the necessary sifting and sorting of longings was not undertaken. Their deepest, most lasting desire for the God, whom they could not acknowledge, nor distinguish from the attraction of something strange and new, led them to the gullible embrace of all that engendered excitement and a pseudo-mysticism. The hard work of submitting one's will to the will of God was substituted by the regimentation and intellectual submission of cult-life that 'softens up anyone for the kill'.

The key to the longings of these seekers is there — known to us; indeed, in our hands. The question is, how do we hold it out? It's an enormous challenge! And yet, in the face of that huge hunger, dare we expend such a colossal amount of energy 'defending our turf' and our rights, focusing on the upkeep of the fabric of the Church and 'keeping the show on the road'?

My eye fell with keen interest on a notice in the classified columns of the *Church Times*[25] in which details were given of a conference to be sponsored by an organisation called 'Christians Awakening to a New Awareness', with the title, 'Thoughts on the Leading Edge of the Church'. I was delighted that some Christians *are* awakening to a new awareness, and I began to ponder what the content of their 'Thoughts . . .' would be. For surely, one essential is that we hear what God is saying to us in this modern era of cultism when, from the 1970s onwards, so many have turned from the Church, where his life and love should be found, and have sought to have their longings met in the astonishing rubble of counter-cultures that have sprung up, such as the

Children of God, the Divine Light Mission, the Church of Scientology, the Unification Church of the Revd Sun Myung Moon, the Vissarion followers based in Siberia, Jim Jones' 'People's Temple', and a whole range of New Age manifestations, devoted to monumental self-concern and self-absorption. And alongside these, occultism has flourished alarmingly.

Miguel de Unamuno asks: 'Do we not naturally believe in that which satisfies our desires?'[26] The answer to that is, 'Only if we have identified the nature of our true desire in the first place.' All too many have been like sheep led astray by false shepherds down false trails. Even allowing that some will jump on the bandwagon of anything that offers novelty or hype, it is a still a terrible indictment on us who have been entrusted with the word of Truth, that it neither appeals to the hearts or minds, nor is received by so many of these 'seekers' of our age.

THREE

TEARS ARE MY FOOD
The Language of Longing

O God, let me rise to the edges of time,
and open my life to your eternity.
Let me run to the edges of space and gaze into your infinity:
Let me climb through the barriers of sound and pass into your silence:
and in stillness let me love and adore you.

Sr Ruth SLG

As soon as we get near the truth of God, our eyes begin to pour
out tears.

Isaac the Syrian

Teresa of Avila once wrote: 'In order to . . . ascend to
the dwelling places we desire, the important thing is not
to think much but to love much; and so do that which
best stirs you to love.'[1]

Her advice is fully in accord with the wisdom of the
Orthodox teaching which speaks of the mind descending
into the heart, to engage in heart language: 'The prin-
cipal thing is to stand with the mind in the heart before
God, and to go on standing before him unceasingly day
and night, until the end of life.'[2]

There have been times in clergy retreats when the
men have admitted that they feel uncomfortable in this

area of the language of longing – indeed, uncomfortable about the longing itself – for possibly a number of reasons, but three in particular seemed to be a problem.

Firstly, they still had an image of God that was predominantly male, and any suggestion that prayer is really a kind of 'holy love-affair' seemed unhealthy and even abhorrent to them.

Secondly, it may be more natural for the majority of men to approach prayer through the mind rather than the feelings. The rational, cognitive, analytical faculties largely come into play. Yet feelings are vital and must have their proper place. Ignatian spirituality has recovered for us some of the importance of being in touch with our feelings and discerning the spirits, i.e. our emotions, in prayer. Decades ago, feelings *were* definitely regarded as suspect, whereas it is dependence on feelings that we have to guard against, not the feelings themselves. When we come to prayer, we bring the whole of ourselves, we can't leave parts behind. In this respect, the Charismatic Movement helped a good many men to own and express their feelings without shame. It takes a very great deal to overcome the legacy of a childhood in which it has been firmly instilled into a boy that 'Boys don't cry!'

Thirdly, my clergy friends told me that they couldn't cope with a language full of sexual overtones and nuptial imagery – despite the fact that they abound in the Scriptures. The references in Hebrew to 'knowing God' and to God 'knowing' his people, carry with them all the intimacy and tenderness of sexual love, which they found acceptable as a piece of linguistic knowledge. But some men, at least, have hang-ups in allowing intimacy and tenderness to become the mainspring of prayer. Possibly any form of intimacy is threatening to them and the fear of it has roots right back in childhood.

Mary Magdalen's reckless, passionate expression of love for Jesus is a symbol for all time of the prayer of longing, but women are likely to identify with it more readily than men. The male onlookers on the occasion of her outpouring of love and tears were desperately embarrassed, as well as critical.[3] I suspect that some contemporary males are often equally so, when it comes to the language of the heart and its expression. The eroticism of the Song of Songs has from time to time raised the question as to whether or not it should ever have been included in the Canon. Yet its images speak powerfully of the contemplative life. It was certainly favoured by the early Fathers and later by Bernard of Clairvaux. When it comes to the language of love and longing at its profoundest, of union with God, we are really lost for any alternative other than nuptial imagery to provide us with a means of expression. In the Middle Ages there was an increasing recourse to the language of love and marriage in what have become the spiritual classics, and the use of sexual imagery to describe union with God was by no means limited to women writers.

These observations are not, of course, the whole story. Some of our most telling and erotic expressions of love-longing for God have come from men – both among the biblical writers and the spiritual Fathers, perhaps very especially John of the Cross,[4] Bernard of Clairvaux, who has been called the Doctor of Love, and Gregory of Nyssa, the 'Theologian of Desire'.

> It depends very much on your point of view whether this [fear of erotic imagery] reflects an unhealthy repression of sexual urges ... or whether that imagery is a perfectly acceptable process of harnessing the power of human desire towards its origin and completion in God. My sense as a historian is that the origins of this language reflect a peculiar mixture of the two.[5]

A stumbling block for all of us in the area of expressing longing is that most of us are out of touch with our primary language. Eugene Peterson points very helpfully to three types of language.[6]

Language 1, he says, is the language of intimacy and relationship – the first one we learn. It consists of much that is not identifiable as intelligent speech. It is what passes between the parent and child and consists of 'coos and cries, that do not parse', 'nonsense syllables that have no dictionary definitions', an exchange of 'gurgles and out-of-tune hums'. As a result of that kind of communication trust develops. The two occasions in life when adults seem not to mind how foolish they sound is, firstly when relating to babies and secondly, when they have fallen in love and resort to highly personalised expressions that would leave an eavesdropper hugely embarrassed.

Language 2 is the language of information – of facts and

details about the world we live in – an objective language. We learn to use sentences and to make connections. It is the language used in education – the language of expanding knowledge.

Language 3 is the language of motivation. We discover that words have the power to make things happen, to move people to strenuous activity on our behalf, to incite people to revolution or revival, to encourage and exhort, to command or dictate. Words can control, whether it be a parent telling a child to 'Be quiet', 'Stop talking while your mouth is full', 'Come out of the bathroom. There's a queue waiting!' or a gangster giving the command, 'Shoot!'. Children quickly learn to be proficient in this language, often grossly manipulating those around them. And in the adult world it is the language used predominantly in advertising and politics.

Clearly languages 2 and 3 dominate our society. 'We are well schooled in language that describes the world in which we live. We are well trained in language that moves people to buy and join and vote.'[7] But would we have to acknowledge that gradually we have grown away from that first language of intimacy? 'Once we are clear of the cradle, we find less and less occasion to use it.'[8] We recover it briefly when we become parents or fall in love – and then slip back into 'normal', comfortable, rational patterns of speech.

And then we wonder why we are stumped when it comes to prayer, for our longings require that we return to Language 1. In prayer we don't need language *about* God but a vehicle by which we can converse with him in loving adoration. We are not looking for *knowledge* about him, but a way of knowing him, intimately, in the secret places of our hearts where we are not afraid to sound ridiculous.

One of the reasons why we may sometimes find the language of the saints and mystics a bit 'sugary' and 'over the top' is precisely because they mostly use Language 1 — the language of relationship, which we, in our 'sophistication' have perhaps inwardly come to despise or distrust. But if we seriously want to commune with God in love-longing, we need to recover it — urgently!

Naming our longings

The question a bishop asks of a Sister or Brother seeking to make his/her profession in life vows in a religious community, is strong and direct. 'N . . . what do you desire?' Though a Sister or Brother responds in a set formula of words, behind them lies a whole hinterland of inner work, of search and self-discovery, of fleshing out the nature of their very personal response and all it implies and demands. The years of novitiate training, the subsequent formation, the days in retreat before profession, the travelling in to the centre of their being, have brought the Brother or Sister to a place where only he or she knows, in his or her heart, *what* exactly the answer to that question could mean. They alone know the depth at which they are capable of responding at that moment.

It is a question each of us might hear the Lord ask of

us. 'What do you desire?' And we may begin our answer, 'I desire . . .' and then find we can get no further. We simply can't find the words to express it. One priest found this to be his experience and wrote the following prayer:

> Lord, I desire, I desire,
> I cannot say how much:
> I only know I stand in need of all things.
> And would that my desire were as great as to my need!
> Lord who alone canst satisfy the human heart's desire,
> And fill with all Thy fullness the abyss of human need,
> Hear now how I desire all good things,
> And Thee, Thyself, my God, above all else,
> Who givest all.[9]

Ignatius of Loyola encouraged what he considered 'a vital prelude' to the beginning of any period of prayer, that is, to ask God for what we want or desire. He would have recognised that, at times, these desires would be fairly superficial. But the aim of the exercise was to help us centre the whole experience of prayer on desire 'in such a way that you could say that desire, understood as an increasing openness to God's possibilities for us, is the essence of our prayer whatever structure or method we adopt'.[10]

The language of longing

To the question, 'How do I express my love-longing for God?' there are nearly as many answers as there are different personalities. Approaches will vary according to individual temperaments.

We can turn to the Psalmists who, because of their emotional honesty, provide us with one of our richest resources for the language of longing. We find ourselves resonating with their aspirations and murmurings of the heart. They manage to voice what for us defies articulation. Our identity as lovers of God is hidden in the Psalms. They speak of silence and stillness, of simply waiting upon God in longing, hope and trust.

> For God alone my soul waits in silence; from him comes my salvation. (Psalm 62:1)

> For God alone my soul waits in silence; for my hope is from him. (Psalm 62:5)

> Be still and know that I am God. (Psalm 46:10)

> O Lord, all my longing is known to you; my sighing is not hidden from you. (Psalm 38:9)

> But it is for you, Lord, that I wait. (Psalm 38:15a)

> I waited patiently for the Lord. (Psalm 40:1a)

> Be still before the Lord and wait patiently for him. (Psalm 37:7a)

> 'Come' my heart says 'seek his face!' Your face, Lord, do I seek. (Psalm 27:8)

> Tarry thou the Lord's leisure. (Psalm 27:14a, Coverdale version)

I will sing of your steadfast love, O Lord, forever; with my mouth I will proclaim your faithfulness to all generations. (Psalm 89:1)

Bless the Lord, O my soul, and all that is within me, bless his holy name. (Psalm 103:1)

My soul languishes for your salvation; I hope in your word. (Psalm 119:81)

I wait for the Lord, my soul waits, and in his word I hope; my soul waits for the Lord more than those who watch for the morning. (Psalm 130:5, 6)

I have calmed and quieted my soul like a weaned child with its mother. (Psalm 131:2)

I love you, O Lord, my strength. The Lord is my rock, my fortress and my deliverer, my God, my rock in whom I take refuge. (Psalm 18:1, 2)

I love the Lord because he has heard my voice and my supplications. Because he inclined his ear to me, therefore I will call on him as long as I live. (Psalm 116:1, 2)

My heart is steadfast, O God, my heart is steadfast; I will sing and make melody. (Psalm 57:7 and Psalm 108:1)

My soul yearns for you in the night; my spirit within me earnestly seeks for you. (Isaiah 26:9)

One can simply wait upon God in a profoundly

satisfying silence – what St Teresa called 'the prayer of quiet' – in stillness and receptivity. It can be refreshing, recreative, nourishing and definitely more-ish! When the Psalmists speak of 'waiting upon God', the word used also means 'longing'. To wait upon the Lord is to be consumed with longing for him. As one writer has put it, it is 'the silent gasp of love that is the Holy Spirit drawing from us an external "Yes" of total surrendering love'.[11] For many of us this silence is evoked by an experience of joy or wonder, for example at the birth of a baby, or when overwhelmed by the natural beauty of some part of creation. 'The eternal silence of those boundless spaces strikes awe into my soul,' wrote Blaise Pascal, and his words would surely find an echo in all our hearts.

Silence is the medium in which our prayer becomes the gaze of the heart, a beholding, nothing but a loving awareness of the Lord. 'I look because I love; I look in order to love, and my love is fed and influenced by looking.'[12]

Or, as James Borst puts it: 'While I am quiet and exist in calm and simple awareness of his presence, my heart gropes towards Him and opens to receive His love. It is a prayer which is wordless, fed by a quiet ardour.'[13] 'By love He can be caught and held, but by thinking never.'[14] There is a darkness which thought and clear knowledge cannot bridge, but only longing love!

Kathleen Norris records her brother as saying in a sermon, 'God's language is silence. How do we translate it?'[15]

In this language of silence, we may use a phrase from the Psalmists as a 'kick start' into a restful waiting on God, but thereafter we can sink into a prayer that needs no words or images. It is simply a loving awareness of God himself; a kindling of an even greater fire of love which warms us inwardly. Though we don't set out consciously to experience warm, cosy feelings in prayer, nevertheless they are given – very occasionally. Richard Rolle, the fourteenth-century mystic, experienced an *actual* warmth around the heart, a physical sensation, as he was absorbed in the gaze of love. He kept feeling his chest – so strong was the sensation of being on fire. Far from being a terrifying experience, however, he found it 'a great and unexpected comfort'.

It may even be, as I frequently find, that it is one word or phrase that launches us into deep contemplative silence. It is as though we possess a whole bunch of keys, and need to know which ones will unlock the doors into contemplation for us. On one occasion, St Francis of Assisi prayed the words, 'My Lord and my God', all night. There are certain 'key words' which are exactly that – *key*, which, when savoured, for me make the silence change colour, as it were, and take on a richer, deeper and more satisfying hue.

Or it may be that a more formal approach is helpful and the Jesus Prayer ('Lord, Jesus Christ, Son of God, have mercy on me, a sinner') or a similar set form of prayer is the 'way in'. We each have to find what works for us.

Secondly, our inner ache for God may give way to a

groaning – a literal, physical groaning, or a groaning in spirit. This may not be a very common experience, but the Psalmist certainly knew it from personal experience. 'Lord, all I long for is before you, and my deep sighing is not hidden from you' (Psalm 38:1).

Jesus knew it – in the Garden of Gethsemane. St Paul speaks of it as 'a sigh too deep for words' (Romans 8:26).

Whenever we open ourselves in prayer to become channels for God to work in and through us, it is the Holy Spirit who is doing the praying – not we. For us it is a matter of making ourselves available, of centring down in loving receptivity and active passivity. And it is from this kenotic passivity, this silent emptying of ourselves, that the Holy Spirit is able to groan in us with 'groanings that cannot be uttered', and intercede through us with 'sighs too deep for words' (Romans 8:26), and, in doing so, 'collect up' our hopes and aspirations, our yearnings for a more intimate relationship with God.

We may sometimes be tempted to think that simply 'beholding the Lord' with a gaze of love-longing is an indulgence. But we cannot possibly measure or anticipate how the Holy Spirit is going to move sovereignly into and through our silence and our loving for his own healing and renewing purposes – to whomever, wherever, whenever he will.

Sometimes our groaning is the only response that rises in us – but we know exactly what has evoked it. It may be connected with what we have read in the paper, or seen on the TV news – the images and scenes of gross violation of human rights, genocidal warfare, poverty and hunger of overwhelming proportions, evidence of cruelty, crime and corruption, the announcement of disastrous decisions that have a global impact. Or it may be a deeper insight into our own sinfulness and our share in the corporate sin of the world, of which we are a part, and therefore can never disown our responsibility.

Jesus enjoined his disciples to 'Watch and pray' and we too may well find that our watching and praying quite literally go together, e.g., with the TV news. Our eyes and ears are instruments that constantly pick up the raw material for intercession. Our reactions of joy, anger, horror, revulsion, delight, compassion etc. in response to all that impinges upon us, are absorbed into and written upon our hearts. And when we come to pray we need only follow the practice of Rabbi Mendel who said, 'The needs of everyone leave a trace in my heart. And when I come to pray I say, "Lord of the Universe, open my heart and read what is therein written".'[16] This points to the broad, all-encompassing nature of prayer in which *everything* that touches us in life registers in our hearts like the pages of a book, and when we open them to the Lord we love, we have no need of words. We invite the Lord to 'Behold and see' what is upon our hearts, and in return, he says to us, 'Behold and see my sorrow, share some of my heartache; but know that your share is "made to measure", fitted to your capacity to suffer (which is always greater than you think), and that it is only an infinitesimal fraction of mine.' Even so, the weight of our tailor-made share in Christ's compassion may give us cause to groan in the Spirit.

For ecstatic praise and thanksgiving, we may be given a 'tongue' (*glossolalia*), flowing out beyond the limitations and restraints of human language. When it comes to adoration, we soon run out of adequate vocabulary. Occasionally a tongue is used, with translation, to speak a prophetic word, or a word of exhortation, which could be conveyed in no other way – perhaps because of our stubborn, 'stiff-necked' hearts that are too hardened to hear it in Scripture, in preaching or in world events. Maybe even less frequently, it is a hallmark of the Spirit's presence and support when, for reasons we may not understand, we are called in prayer to some form of spiritual warfare, 'to go down into the pit' (Psalm 28:1), to be led into deeper insight and knowledge of the sheer enormity of wickedness that permeates this world, the depth of its depravity, and its source in hell; when we are drawn to be alongside tormented souls in their lost-ness, their emotional or mental agony.

The language of tears

Perhaps the most neglected language of longing (in the Western Church, at any rate) is that of tears. It has for long had an important place in the Eastern tradition where they speak of it as 'the gift of tears'. It is indeed a gift and nothing of which to be ashamed. But it can be startling and maybe embarrassing if one is not aware of this particular work of the Spirit. The tears need no explanation, they are a language in themselves. The Psalmist said: 'My tears have been my meat day and night, while they ask me all day long, "Where is now your God?" ' (Psalm 42:3). This is a direct reference to the nourishing power of tears. The experience of this gift can continue to sustain the soul with life-giving energy for years to come.

It is not simply weeping in sorrow for sin – though there is a strong element of that in it. Nor is it just weeping for joy – though there is that in it too. It is far more a convergence of a desperate yearning, a terrible longing for God, and a piercing sorrow for the sin that 'wounds his love and mars his image in us'.[17] Such an experience of 'piercing' was referred to by the early Fathers as *compunction*, and early religious art often sought to depict it in the form of saints swooning on couches with an arrow piercing (puncturing) the breast, released from a bow held by an angel or cherub lurking somewhere overhead. We may find such imagery somewhat sickly and sentimental, but we need to be tolerant of the rather specialised artistic and linguistic symbols of a former age. For symbols are necessary and, perforce, *contemporary*, because reality is so much larger than anything we can grasp cerebrally. 'Symbols bind up reality for us',[18] and are a way of mediating the inexpressible – but in each generation they need demythologising. Behind them lies a substantial truth that remains for us to discover, and in such a gift as 'tears', we feel a real touch of God. But it is a gift. We can be open to receive it, but can never demand or artificially engineer it. It is given solely at God's discretion. And the timing is his, too. The tears may flow for minutes or hours, but in compunction there is no awareness of the passage of time, only of being more and more deeply cleansed until one emerges feeling 'rinsed' through and through. That is because,

> at some unanticipated point in this process of experiencing one's interior brokenness and alien- ation from God, one's hardness of heart through years of bitterness and hatred, and one's pride and indifference to God's loving call to share his happi- ness and his life the individual at last has an experience of a heart of stone being replaced by a heart of flesh (Ezekiel 36:26).[19]

Thomas Merton knew this kind of experience. He wrote:

> I spent the time in prayer and came out feeling as if I had been pierced and baptised and with new knowledge about prayer – and, I hope, humility, as if I had passed some milestone and gone down lower, or, if you prefer, up higher, or at least out of myself.[20]

That sums it up exactly – 'a going out of oneself'. The tears of grief burst forth only because there is such a deep yearning for God, and the more we yearn, the more we are enlightened about the sin that stands in the way of our growing in his likeness – the decep- tion, the lies, the fears, the anxieties, the compulsions, the cruelties, the sloth and depravity, the sins of the body and the sins of the imagination, the power lust, the greed, the self-centredness, the pride, and all the attempts to be 'as God', in all manner of situations. As Isaac the Syrian has said, 'As soon as we get near the truth of God our eyes begin to pour out tears.'

This is not hysteria. The 'piercing' of compunction is not chiefly to provoke guilt but to stimulate new desire. We are drawn to God far more by gratitude than guilt. 'Yet our ingrained habits and addictive emotions need to be pierced through; we need to be inspired by new prospects and higher standards of what a holy and godly life entails.'[21] True compunction touches us at the very core of our being, and changes us, softens our hearts, makes us more vulnerable but receptive to the Holy Spirit's work. 'Don't be afraid to go soft,' Ronald Rolheiser exhorts us, 'redemption lies in tears. Resist the macho impulse; the person who will not have a softening of the heart will eventually have a softening of the brain.'[22]

It is possible to imitate the gift (as indeed some have done over the gift of tongues when they felt that without the manifestation of that particular gift, they would be deemed 'second-class Christians'). Climacus refers to some of the neurotic people he met who attempted to 'engineer' the gift, some struggling to squeeze out a few tears and others weeping copiously – but, in both cases, spuriously. 'I have seen small tear drops shed with difficulty like drops of blood, and I have seen fountains of tears poured out without difficulty. And I judged these toilers more by their toil than by their tears, and I think God does too.'[23]

The more we long for reality, for 'truth in the inward being' (Psalm 51:6) the more we will predispose ourselves for the gift. Gregory of Nyssa said, 'It is impossible for one to live without tears who considers things exactly as they really are.'[24]

It is when that deep desire to face reality meets head on with a longing for God that is purely for him – pruned of all self-seeking, any desire for greater spiritual gifts, or spiritual growth, but wants only God himself – that the spirit is overwhelmed and tears flow. Rather like the meeting of the Atlantic and Indian oceans at the Cape of Good Hope – when two oceans of love-longing meet, there is much (turbulent) water!

Baptism of tears?

Some refer to this gift as the 'baptism of tears' – a baptism not by water but by the Holy Spirit. Certainly it would be true to say that it is like a total immersion in God's steadfast love and mercy. It is an ongoing conversion bringing with it a liberating joy and sense of his comfort. When our desires have been truly purified, there is an abiding sense of inner serenity and happiness – though that purification must always be continuous. In that the gift of tears has within it the movement from death to resurrection, the experience of being 'raised to newness of life' (Romans 6:4) which is fundamental to baptism, then the description, 'baptism of tears', would be apt. But it carries with it the risk of misunderstanding. For Paul also states that there is 'One Lord, One faith and *one baptism*'. Our baptism may have been in water, but at the same time, it was a baptism of the Spirit. Try leaving him out! Any further experiences of the Spirit's gifts are not fresh baptisms, but an outworking and fulfilling of our original baptism, a deeper appropriation of the potential given us in that sacrament, a further entering into the dying/rising principle which is at the heart of our baptismal vocation. Groaning, tongues and tears, then, are not separate baptisms but a continuing one. At different stages in our lives, the Spirit comes to unwrap more of the gifts that we received in seed at our baptism and encourages us to use and enjoy them. Our ongoing inner work is to appropriate them and offer them back in service to God and his people. Tears are not morbid. They are a very great grace in prayer. They lead to a new inner freedom and a new sense of God's compassion – for us and for all humanity. 'Let your heart become the place where the tears of God and the tears of God's children merge and become the tears of hope.'[25]

Different symbols and expressions we may use, but as for the early Fathers so for the Christian of the 'cybernetic society of the twentieth century',[26] there is a need to enter ever more deeply into our baptism, which indeed happened at one particular point in our lives, but which is an ongoing grace of growing 'in Christ' and a continuing and profound penetration into the mystery of his passion and resurrection. The mystical meaning of

baptism is not always a vibrant reality in the lives
of individual Christians. Its centrality in our faith and
commitment is not always recognised. But a deeper grasp
of its significance, a desire to live it more fully and
celebrate it more often, will bring with it a recreating
force in our lives, an ever intensifying longing for God,
and a variety of Spirit-given ways of expressing that
longing.

FOUR

NEVER SATISFIED
The Insatiability of Longing

> Sometimes you will taste and see how good the Lord is.
> Be glad then, and give him all the honour,
> because his goodness to you has no measure.
> Sometimes you will be dry and joyless
> like parched land or an empty well.
> But your thirst and your helplessness
> will be your best prayer
> if you accept them with patience
> and embrace them lovingly.
> . . . Sometimes you will be able to pray
> only with your body and hands and eyes;
> Sometimes your prayer will move beyond words and images.
>
> Rule for a New Brother (Taizé)

The withholding of satisfaction

Why, we might wonder, does God implant in us a deep desire for himself, an all-consuming longing, and then not satisfy it fully, freely and at once? Unquestionably, the longing of our hearts is matched by his. 'He is', as Maria Boulding has it, 'on the inside of our longings.'[1] He loves us to long for him, but when we do, he leaves us not only unsatisfied, but often desolate.

Sometimes it feels as though he is playing a kind of

'hide and seek' with us as the Beloved did with the Lover in the Song of Songs. Appearing at the window fleetingly, knocking on it and then vanishing, the elusive Beloved seems to amuse himself with maddeningly childish tricks until, eventually, the distraught woman can contain her despair no longer and goes flying round the streets asking all and sundry, 'Have you seen him whom my soul loves?' She determines to 'seek him whom her soul loves' and when she finds him, 'never to let him go' (Song of Songs 2).

There are times in prayer when many of us could identify with that desperation, when we long for some small manifestation of God's presence, a fresh experience of his love, a knock on the window of our soul – and we are faced with an awful nothingness, seemingly no response, no reciprocal desire for communion. All down through the ages, holy men and women have experienced this strange absenteeism in God. They knew all about these contrasts of God's coming and going, of the finding and losing, the joy and sadness that we know so well. The Psalmists' and the Prophets' anguish often resonates powerfully with our own.

Do not hide your face from me. (Psalm 102:2a)

My soul languishes for your salvation . . . my eyes fail with watching for your promise; I ask, 'When will you comfort me?' (Psalm 119:81a, 82)

Satisfy us in the morning with your steadfast love . . . (Psalm 90:14a)

72

How long O Lord? Will you hide yourself for
ever? . . . Where is your steadfast love of old? (Psalm
89:46a and 49a)

O Lord, why do you cast me off? Why do you hide
your face from me? (Psalm 88:14)

Truly, you are a God who hides himself. (Isaiah
45:15a)

Where are your zeal and your might? The yearning
of your heart and your compassion? They are with-
held from me? (Isaiah 63:15b)

Why is it that God leaves us to struggle in yawning
chasms of desolation instead of taking us to heights
of consolation? Is it unreasonable to hope for some
encouragement, rather than to suffer a sense of abandon-
ment? Is it improper to expect some degree of
satisfaction for our longing?

'To find God', said Gregory of Nyssa, 'is to seek him
unceasingly. Here, indeed, to seek is not one thing and
to find another. The reward of the search is to go on
searching. The soul's desire is fulfilled by the very fact
of its remaining unsatisfied. For really to see God is
never to have had one's fill of desiring him.'[2]

We have already seen that those 'seekers' of our own
day who have turned to various cults were prompted by
deep and immemorial longings for which they could
not begin to find true satisfaction here and now, and
therefore decided it could only be attained in a life
beyond. They sought – they knew not what or whom.

They looked in the wrong direction, so did not make the discovery which is the common experience in Christian contemplation – that seeking and finding are not two opposites. Paradoxically they go hand in hand. For, although our hearts cry out, as did the woman in the Song of Songs, and as Mary Magdalen did in her seeming loss, there is nevertheless a throbbing, dynamic life in the longing itself. It keeps us stretching and yearning, embracing and valuing our longing. We have no urge to abandon it. On the contrary, it is heightened by the very fact that it is not answered. 'Holy desires grow by delay,' said Gregory the Great.[3]

The pain of losing and finding

Even with this understanding, our desert experiences of desolation can be times of immense suffering – but a suffering which also intensifies our longing for God.

> And our presumption in expecting God to act in our time rather than his, is eliminated if we are as content to wait for him in the 'dark night of the soul' as in the broad daylight of God's embrace. It will only be after death that this interplay of absence and presence will finally be over. In this world, human beings require the changing movements of desire to continue throughout life.[4]

Speaking of Mary Magdalen's panic-stricken need to search for her missing Lord on discovering the empty tomb, Bernard of Clairvaux reminds us that it is a search we must all pursue if we truly desire him: 'Never despair of finding him . . . Seek him by desire, follow him through action, and in faith you will find him . . . He can never be sought in vain, even when we cannot find him.'[5]

Our conscious motives for seeking and finding him will vary at different stages of our pilgrimage through the 'desert'. Just as Mary Magdalen at the tomb had to learn not to cling neurotically to Jesus in the old pre-resurrection relationship, had to 'let go' her need to enshrine him in the known and familiar, so we too may have to 'let go' some of our presuppositions, our preconceived expectations of how we will encounter him. We are constantly having to die to what would trap us in an immature, static relationship, in order to be free to explore the new dimensions that he 'goes before' to prepare for us. Without the constant correction of our desires, we would be in danger of settling down too easily to 'a degenerate and sentimental self-sufficiency, convinced that we had arrived'.[6] There would be the danger of stagnating spiritually, or of imagining that the ascent was over. Once more, Gregory of Nyssa illuminates this for us.

> It always seems to the soul as though it is only at the beginning of the ascent. That is why the Lord repeats, 'Arise' to one who is already arisen; 'Come' to the one who has already come. He who truly rises will always have to rise; there will always be a great distance to run for him who is running towards the

Lord. Thus he who climbs can never cease from climbing, going from fresh beginning to fresh beginning – beginnings which never have an end.[7]

Reasons for denying us complete satisfaction of our longings

Sometimes God withholds delights lest satisfaction should become the cause of pride. In their journeying, the people of Israel appealed to God as protector and provider. But when they began to embrace other gods beside him, the Lord had to rebuke them. 'You know no God but me, and besides me there is no Saviour . . . when I fed them, they were satisfied; they were satisfied and their heart was proud; therefore they forgot me' (Hosea 13:4b, 6).

If God were to grant our desire for spiritual riches – for perhaps some gift of deeper prayer or insight – pride might lead us to flaunt or to exhibit the gift in a kind of spiritual one-upmanship which would exalt us rather than him. Then, in sadness, God would have to say to us, 'I satisfied them and their heart was proud. Having heard their cries and granted their requests, they simply forgot me and focused on the gift, not the Giver.'

Merton was very aware of this danger of wanting to 'show off' God's gifts and thus enhance our own image. He wrote:

God does not tell his purest secrets to one who is prepared to reveal them. He has secrets which he

tells to those who will communicate some idea of
them to others. But these secrets are the common
property of many. He has other secrets which cannot
be told. The mere desire to tell them makes us
incapable of receiving them. The greatest of God's
secrets is God himself. He waits to communicate
himself to me in a way that I can never express to
others, or even think about coherently to myself. I
must desire in silence.[8]

Not only is the withholding of the satisfaction of our
desires in order that our growth may not be stunted or
our hearts proud, God may well, in his wisdom, choose
to take us through the 'furnace of adversity' in order to
refine our longings and purge the pride that would claim
the glory for ourselves. 'For my own sake I do it . . .'
says the Lord, 'my glory I will not give to another'
(Isaiah 48:10, 7, 11a).

Cardinal Basil Hume observes: 'It is better to walk
through darkness, the Lord guiding you, than to sit
enthroned in light that radiates from yourself.'[9]

We have to learn indifference to consolation or desolation and accept that both will come our way as a
normal part of our spiritual journey. Feelings are greatly
involved, and feelings are notoriously unreliable. In Ignatius of Loyola's terms (cf. *The Spiritual Exercises*, 316)
spiritual consolation is every increase of faith, hope and
love, and a quiet awareness and interior joy in which
our affectivity is so captured by the love of God that
everything is experienced in relation to him. Spiritual

desolation is a darkness of soul and turmoil of spirit, a restlessness arising from many inner disturbances and temptations which lead to a diminishment of faith, hope and love. The soul is tepid and sad and feels separated from its Lord. We need to distinguish carefully between desolation and those states which spring from a physical or psychological context. Most depression is not desolation. Desolation has far more to do with those times when the heart desires God and the feelings don't.

We are likely to experience more times of desolation than consolation, for strangely our capacity for joy is far more limited than that for suffering. Every period of desolation is an invitation to discover more of 'the treasures of darkness' of which Isaiah speaks (Isaiah 45:3), and it is from this 'storehouse' that truths are communicated to us that could be revealed in no other way.

I have already considered some of those 'treasures' fairly fully in *Jesus, Man of Prayer*,[10] but here would like to unwrap a few more.

Darkness can be a time both of growth and resting. In natural terms they go together. It is while we sleep that the body grows, during sleep that the vital organs are continually being renewed, fresh cells replacing those that have died.

Ordinarily, when we grope around in the dark we have to rely on senses other than sight − touch, sound, smell. Similarly, in the spiritual life, when 'sight' is denied us, our faith is honed to a keener cutting edge, and our hope becomes certainty. Such darkness then is pure blessing. Why is it that so many of us like to pray in a darkened chapel or room – or maybe by the light of a single candle? There is a sense in which the darkness focuses us, enables us to gather ourselves, wrap ourselves within its folds and form an inner enclosure where nothing and no one can intrude. Dazzled by too much light of knowledge and too great a sense of consolation, we become distracted and eccentric (literally: drawn away from the centre). Whereas in the darkness of our senses, we are strangely aware of that all-pervading Presence, just as surely as we know when someone has entered our darkened room, no matter how stealthily.

Furthermore some gems only reveal their full beauty in the dark, when they glow with inner light. And there are those truths which are like cats' eyes. In the blackness, all unbidden, we suddenly see them. In the light of consolation we would barely notice them – for the brighter the light the more they close up!

In his book *The Heart of the World* Alan Ereira tells how he was allowed to stay over a period of three years with a very remarkable tribe of people, the Kogi, who for centuries have lived in deliberate isolation from the rest of the world, supporting themselves, upholding an ancient culture and a lost civilisation. A priesthood still rules over the communities and they safeguard a way of life that honours the balance of life on earth between humanity, nature and the spiritual world. Their priests could more aptly be described as the wise men of the community. They do not preside at worship or offer sacrifices, and they are not referred to as priests, but Mamas. One of the most astonishing practices of the

Kogi is their training of a Mama. He is selected at birth and immediately taken to a cave or darkened house where he is never permitted to see the light. His mother is allowed to go in each day and feed and bathe him and he has a tutor who is responsible for his care. He is only ever allowed out at night – and even then wearing a straw hat to prevent him from seeing the moon and the stars. Amazingly in his life of darkness with no knowledge of the outer world, no formal teaching, no childhood friends with whom to play, he actually begins to sing – spontaneously. The reason for this extra-ordinary training is that in *the dark* the infant Mama becomes more attuned to the world of the spirit. The child who has been reared in the spirit world begins to hear the inner music of the universe and acts in accord-ance with what he hears. He begins to dance. By keeping his contact with the material world to an absolute minimum, the child's mind is raised to a level of vastly heightened awareness, a state of raised consciousness. Eventually after years of darkness in which the mind, the senses and the spirit have been tuned to a degree of vibrant sensitivity, the young Mama emerges to take his place in the community.

The Mama with the most profound understanding is the Mama who speaks with the greatest simplicity. There is a kind of state of grace, which the whole community recognises, which some truly great Mamas achieve. It is seen sometimes fleetingly . . . in ecstatic understanding produced when the Mamas fast and go without sleep for days and nights on end, but in some special individuals it becomes the way they are. These people have, as it were, stepped through the limitations of human understanding. They become like children, the world is ever fresh to them. They understand their own ignorance. These are, to the Kogi, the wisest people.[11]

Our experiences of darkness in the spiritual life are not likely to be as radical or rigorous as that of a Mama in training. Even so, they may well be the means by which we are able to 'step through the limitations of human understanding' and rational knowledge into a realm where we are far more sensitively attuned to the movements of the Spirit as we walk by faith and not by sight.

We may discover another of the 'treasures of darkness' to be a more radical experience of God's mercy. The apparent withdrawal of light, our inability to see and know, is because we would be blinded by too much brilliance. The writers of the apophatic tradition, among whom Gregory of Nyssa was a leading exponent, and later, St John of the Cross, spoke of the 'way of darkness' or 'the via negativa'. They taught that the light of God in the soul is sometimes experienced as darkness. Dazzling darkness, they called it. Our temporary blindness is not due to an absence of light but an excess of it. In this dazzling darkness divine things are given to believers.

Now Christ is calling you to let go of your controlled thinking . . . and to surrender in deeper faith, hope and love to his indwelling presence, beyond any feeling you may have . . . Christ is calling you into deeper darkness, the darkening of your own rational knowledge, to enter into a new way of receiving the communication of himself in the 'darkness' of faith.[12]

If we embrace the darkness as a merciful gift, we will be truly grateful for it. If we accept it as absolutely the right soil in which our faith will grow, then the absence of any sensible, felt presence of the Lord will be a 'severe mercy'.

> To pray in the absence of God, to know that he is there but I am blind; that he is there but I am insensitive and it is an act of his infinite mercy not to be present to me while I am not yet capable of sustaining his coming . . . if only we could appreciate, could be grateful to God for his absence which teaches us to knock at the door, to test our thoughts and hearts, to consider the significance of our actions, to appraise the impulses of our whole being, to ask ourselves whether our will is really orientated towards God or, if we look to God for a moment's respite from our burdens, only to forsake him the next instant, as soon as we have recovered our strength, to squander that energy he has given us like the prodigal son.[13]

If we *could* be thankful when he withholds satisfaction from us and befriend the darkness, we would begin to discover more and more of its treasures. For it is not for us to call the shots. We have to let *God* judge when, in our best interests, we should be plunged into darkness and when we are capable of greater insight and more dazzling illumination.

Seeking the face of God

'My heart has said, "Seek his face." Your face Lord I will seek' (Psalm 27:8, 9). 'Seeking the face of God' features large in the Old Testament writings, particularly those of the Psalmists, and is the poignant counterpart to God's apparent hiding of his face, his reluctance to disclose himself prematurely.

'My soul longs for your salvation: when shall I come to see your face?' (i.e. to know you more intimately) is a response with a haunting tune, sung in our Community, in which words and music together have the power to touch the heart directly and move it into deeper dimensions of longing. In response to our plea to know the nature of God more fully, we may be granted a succession of dimly perceived and passing images. We cannot behold the face of God fully in this life, but each fragmentary disclosure fuels our desire further. We tend to ache after what is beyond our grasp – but it keeps us straining forward eagerly. For the vision of God in this life is discipleship. It is perfectly right and proper to pray with Moses, 'Show me your glory', provided we also are prepared to be drawn into a cleft where we can only apprehend him from behind as our hearts follow him in love. It is essential that we bring our longings, desires and emptiness into our prayers, as our 'fast God' forges ahead, ever drawing us into fresh 'clefts in the rock', new 'gaps' where we will suddenly glimpse his glory passing by, 'going before us' and beckoning us on. 'Desire drives us beyond the safe and manageable to "stalk the gaps" ' and leap from cleft to cleft.[14]

Gregory of Nyssa has been called a theologian of desire. He is persuaded that,

> Hope always draws the soul from beauty which is seen to what is beyond, always kindles the desire for the hidden through what is constantly perceived . . . And the bold request [of Moses] which goes up the mountains of desire asks this: to enjoy the Beauty not in mirrors and reflections, but face to face.[15]

Gregory's own search for God seems to have been fed more by desire than by a certitude of faith, writes Kathleen Norris. 'I frequently take consolation in Gregory's sense that with God there is always more unfolding, that what we can glimpse of the divine is always enough, and never enough.'[16]

We should feel glad that our longings are never completely satisfied in this life, that we are always left with what Augustine called 'the blind pull of desire'. Our hunger for God will increase in exact proportion to the depth of our longing. For the 'appetite grows by what it feeds on'. We will always have gnawing spiritual pangs to 'taste Thee, O Thou Living Bread and long to feast upon Thee still'.[17] We will constantly be consumed with a raging thirst that sends us flying to drink from the fountain which alone will begin to fill our souls. Bernard of Clairvaux had his finger right on the pulse of spiritual desire when he wrote these words. They have been a source of devotional inspiration to generations of Christians.

Of course, it may be that our longings simply lack energy. We are not sufficiently 'children of the burning heart'.[18] We are lethargic by comparison with the heat of desire experienced by holy men and women of the past. In the light of their passion and zeal our desires seem to have become tamed and domesticated. The furnace of our heart needs to be refuelled with a torrent of desire, as David's was as he sang his Psalms, and as Paul's was when he could claim that his only goal was, 'that I may know him'. It was *that* towards which he was pressing forward eagerly and unrestrainedly. Our desires often become submerged in a welter of externals, but Paul's priorities were such that he regarded everything as loss because of the surpassing worth of knowing Christ Jesus, his Lord. For his sake, Paul was prepared to suffer the loss of all things and to regard them as rubbish, in order to gain Christ and be found in him (Philippians 3:8).

To what extent could that be our claim? Are our desires zestful enough to keep us following the Lord with an undivided heart, grateful that they are not so fully met that we are overwhelmed; not so fully met that we stop pressing forward eagerly? And is the bottom line in all our desiring a passionate love of the Lord that is neither checked by darkness nor subdued into complacency by light? 'Are we still fired into life by a madness which lets us understand the insatiability of our hearts as a call to infinite love?'[19]

Lord,

> I offer what I am
> to what You are.
> I stretch up to You in desire
> my attention on You alone.
> I cannot grasp You
>> explain You
>> describe You
> Only cast myself into the depths
>> of your mystery.
> Only let Your love pierce
>> the cloud of my unknowing.
> Let me forget all but You.
> You are what I long for.
> You are my chiefest good.
> You are my eager hope.
> You are my allness.

> In the glimpse of Your Eternity,
>> Your unconditional Freedom,
>> Your Perfect Love,
> I am humble and worshipping,
>> warming to love and hope,
>> waiting and available
>> for Your Will
>>> dear Lord.[20]

FIVE

THE WOUND OF LOVE

The Abyss of Longing

They shall look on him whom they have pierced . . .

Zechariah 12:10b

Heart of our God and our desire,
Strike from our flint your spark of fire.
Give us yet more than gift unpriced,
A share in your compassion Christ![1]

Sr Janet CSMV

Jesus, grant me this I pray,
Ever in Thy heart to stay;
Let me ever there abide,
Hidden in Thy wounded side.[2]

Each year as we celebrate the Feast of the Sacred Heart and sing the words of the above hymn, I find myself wondering if we have any idea of the enormity of our request.

To share in Christ's compassion is to know, to an intensely raw degree, the very heartache of God – a rending heartache which is the price he pays for being all love. To be lover and creator inevitably brings a supremely heavy load of suffering. Even for us as human beings, to see something we have created out of love destroyed before our eyes is one of the most searing of all pains. That holds for any fruit of our creativity whether it be artistic, literary, an organisation, the building up of a company or community project which may have been the result of a lifetime's service. When our works of art are stolen or slashed, our creative writing ripped to pieces by critics, our ventures thwarted and our projects brought to nought, part of us dies too.

But to see the 'fruit of one's *body*' destroyed, brings with it a 'death' before death – beyond all imagining, except for those who have suffered such a loss.

Mary gave birth to the One who was to be Saviour of humanity, and was forewarned by Simeon that her child, the fruit of her own creativity and obedience, was 'destined for the falling and rising of many in Israel'. He was to be a 'sign that will be opposed so that the inner thoughts of many will be revealed – and a sword will pierce your own soul, too' (Luke 2:35). Mary must surely have noted that 'too' – it implied a sword for the Son, and a sword for his mother. Quite certainly, Mary would gladly have borne a *double* sword-thrust, if it could have spared her Son.

Any parent who has lost a son or daughter (at whatever age) will confirm that there is no pain to be compared with it. Did Mary ever know just how many other swords pierced countless other sons, and their mothers, because hers had been born into the world, and constituted a threat to an insanely jealous Tetrarch?

Here in South Africa, there are vast numbers of

mothers, who, like Mary, have actually witnessed the murder of their sons and daughters, been forced to watch them being tortured to death. In a unique way, they are able to enter into Mary's suffering and she into theirs. They know, from the inside, the powerlessness she felt as she stood at the foot of the cross whilst her Son died one of the most cruel and protracted deaths human beings have ever devised. She entered, too, into his pain of rejected love. But nothing could break that power of love or cause him to deviate from it for one moment. No matter what evil was hurled at him, he met it only with love. Evil has no answer to that!

If we as human beings know, from personal experience, something of the agony of the creator, as our workmanship is misused, abused or devastated, and know too the intolerable suffering of standing powerlessly by as a son or daughter dies, perhaps we can begin to comprehend how immeasurable must be the suffering of a Creator God when he looks on the damage humanity has inflicted on his creation since the beginning of time, and the wreckage each generation has left in its wake; when he grieves over the sheer, unfathomable evil we have unleashed upon the world, and enters into the crucifixion of his only Son in order to reconcile that estranged world to himself.

Much of that evil is now so commonplace in our society that we have succumbed to a psychic numbness which softens the shock waves of sorrow and horror. We sometimes feel we have reached the point of compassion fatigue and can bear no more. So, we are tempted to 'switch off' our emotions and spare ourselves the pain of knowing the *extent* of the appalling weight of suffering in the world. Or the media's constant and almost exclusive focus on crime and disaster, cruelty and corruption, begins to build up in us a kind of immunity born of over-familiarity. But woe to us if we allow ourselves to be thus anaesthetised – however much suffering it may save us. For God, in his love, grieves ever more intensely, looks upon his wounded world with a breaking heart, enters into the brokenness of humanity with inexhaustible compassion, and invites us to share in it with him. Nothing can make him a less loving God, but much can make him a more suffering one.

'While Earth wears wounds, still must Christ's wounds remain,' wrote Lawrence Housman.[3] He still weeps over the cities of the world that do not know the things that belong to their peace, and those tears once shed through his own human body have now to be incarnated through us. We become the irrigation channels through which his tears water the earth's wounds in healing and mercy.

To share in the compassion of Christ is to know 'that internal rending called "the broken heart" '. Those who respond to the invitation to share that compassion, whose sensitivity is acutely honed, will not

> live long in this world before they have their hearts broken. Then, as life goes on, the broken heart will be further sundered into smaller and even smaller pieces. This is especially the case, of course, with

those who deliberately seek union with him in his Passion . . . However, they also come to know that without any question, the important thing is to let the world break the human heart. For one thing, there is room in the broken heart – and only there – for all the sorrows of the world. The broken heart – and only it – is curative, redemptive, of the wasteland around. In addition, it is the new raw material necessary for a strange and important alchemy which has been described in the words: 'Your sorrow shall be turned into joy' (John 16:20).[4]

For it is the concomitant of resurrection life, and as Tony Campolo has said,

resurrection life is not about having wonderful spiritual experiences of joy and worship, or speaking in tongues, victorious praying, or seeing dramatic healings and visions (though they have their place). To be filled with the Spirit is to have your heart broken by the same things that broke Jesus' heart.[5]

Trevor Hudson has a saying that Jesus comes into our lives not to make us feel good, but to feel *more*.[6]

Do we then dare pray, 'Give us yet more that gift unpriced, a share in your compassion, Christ'? Or do we actually shrink from so demanding a gift and seek escape by becoming compulsive 'do-gooders', frantically trying to control and manipulate situations in order to ensure that we keep the pain at a manageable distance, rushing around imagining ourselves to be the Saviour, instead of co-operating with the Saviour in his divine compassion? For compassion by very definition denotes suffering.

It is all too easy to confuse compassion with doing good and they are not necessarily the same. Gerald May speaks of 'addictive helpfulness' and points to the need to consider 'a little abstinence from automatic reflexive responses of being helpful to others. To do so may require us to examine the ways in which we habitually express love, and that comes close to challenging the love itself.'[7]

When we are brought face to face with the suffering of another, sympathy wells up in us; we want to help – which is fine. But when we begin to put desire into action, our addictions of helpfulness are triggered off.

> In a very computer-like way, our internal pro-grammes of what-to-do-in-a-situation-like-this are accessed and run. In a very uncomputer-like way, we don't even take the time to see which programme is called for. There is no time. We must be about the business of being helpful.[8]

It is far from easy to enter into another's pain, to em-pathise, simply to 'be there' and stay with the pain. But we need to honour that small gap between feeling a person's pain and leaping into action. For in that space we have the chance to listen to what they really need, to listen to the Lord whose compassion it is that we invite to flow through us, and to discern how he would want us to incarnate and express it.

The 'Beware!' signs are everywhere crying out to be heeded if we are to become, with Christ, the 'burden bearers of creation'.[9] Jumping into our inveterate 'helping role' is possibly our unconscious way of trying to minimise the raw agony of feeling someone else's pain and of coping with the fear that too much identification with the suffering of others, too much compassion, will lead to burn-out. But we can be reassured. It isn't feeling the pain of others that leads to burn-out, but our frenzied, compulsive need to be doing good all the time. 'We burn out because we don't allow ourselves space between feeling and response.'[10]

Space is essential if the pain and the tears of compassion are to be 'collected', gathered up, and allowed to flow back to the Lord who himself inspired them in us in the first place. If they get blocked in us then indeed it could lead to burn-out or breakdown. Minds and emotions can fracture under such stress.

Sensitivity will demand that we curb our 'addictive helpfulness' and stand back in unobtrusive sympathy, listening with full attention of heart and mind to the needs of the other – to the body language, the silences, the tears, and also to our own feelings – alert and ready to respond in whatever way is asked of us, but not simply in the way we may have predetermined. It means setting aside our own agenda, our need to be needed, our need to 'get it right' – to be sure we have said the appropriate word or offered the acceptable gesture of comfort. We fear being found wanting in our attempts to minister. It is never easy to be 'useless' or to be

thought 'uncaring'. It is uncomfortable to feel unsure of
the right course of action. Simply to leave someone alone
in their pain, to remain silent and inactive when the
situation seems to scream for action, may seem like
failure. It may send us off on a guilt-trip. It certainly
doesn't do much for our egos! But then, compassion is
not about achievement or making a good impression. It
is not concerned with personal credit. It is a selfless
listening with the whole of our being, a deeply sensitive
receptivity and a quiet empathy with the other. Our
inactivity may well be the greatest mercy we could show
to them.

'Authentic, loving responsiveness calls for a kind of
fasting from being helpful. Real helpfulness requires a
relinquishment of our caretaking reflexes. It demands
that we stay present with the unanaesthetised pain of the
person or situation, but that we also risk appearing to
be uncaring'[11] and unsure what to do.

Sometimes just 'being there' in silent, loving attention
is the most compassionate thing we can do. In 1993,
during the violence that preceded the elections in South
Africa, it was very moving, night after night on the TV
news, to see how wherever strife and killings broke out
in the township communities, the Church was there –
represented by bishops, ministers and leaders. Few
realised the extent of the risks they took and the conse-
quent toll upon their wives and families. After two
massacres on Table Mountain in Natal, we saw scenes of
Archbishop Desmond Tutu and Bishop Michael Nuttall
(Bishop of Natal) visiting the bereaved families of victims

both from the initial attack on a school bus, and a few days later from a reprisal attack – listening to their stories and praying with them. After the assassination of Chris Hani, Bishop David Beetge (Bishop of the Diocese of the High Veld) and ministers of other denominations were filmed walking to the Hani home to offer sympathy and pray with the family – no matter that Chris Hani had been leader of the Communist Party. Compassion does not set boundaries. One of the clergy wives stayed all day with Mrs Hani – just to be there and, by her presence, to offer comfort.

In that situation of seething political and racial tension, church leaders were there, in the thick of the troubles, to show solidarity of sorrow, to offer comfort quite impartially, and to pray with the mourners. There was very little practically that they could do. But they assisted by their presence. What must it have meant to the parents of those children to know that Archbishop Desmond had flown up especially from Cape Town simply in order to be alongside them in their grieving?

Often a member of a royal family, a Prime Minister or President, will hasten to visit a disaster area or the scene of a major tragedy. And one might wonder what point there is, since there is little they can actually do except talk with the wounded, the survivors and the bereaved. Yet, somehow it matters to the people involved that the leaders of a nation are there as its representatives showing concern and compassionate solidarity on behalf of all by their presence.

The French verb *assister* doesn't mean 'to help', but simply 'to attend', to be there, to be present.

I discovered during my years in Botswana that people travel vast distances, no matter how costly or inconvenient, to attend, to be present at, a funeral. Culturally, funerals are one of the most important events in life! From the perspective of my present age, I cannot think what induced me to hitch-hike from college and sleep on the pavement by the Cenotaph in London, to be near Westminster Abbey for the Coronation of Queen Elizabeth II. I would have seen far more had I stayed in our hall of residence and watched it on a borrowed TV. But it is a strange urge 'to be there' that presses upon us at all sorts of turns in life. Any football or pop fan will confirm that it isn't at all the same, just being a passive TV spectator.

'Assistance' means not simply 'going to' but 'staying with', and maybe this is a helpful image to bear in mind as we seek to discover ever more deeply what it means to 'share the compassion of Christ'. If we see it as 'assisting' him, being present to him, simply by being there before him in silent attention and love, we can be assured that we are sharing in his sorrow for his suffering world. Compassion is the ultimate power of God and indeed of humanity, according to Hildegard of Bingen, and Meister Eckhart said: 'You may call God love; you may call God goodness; but the best name for God is Compassion'[12] – and we are 'called by his name' (Jeremiah 14:9b).

The memory of those bishops in their purple cassocks

standing amongst the township mourners in their hour
of grieving provided a striking picture of what we do
when we intercede. We cannot always be physically
present to those caught up in tragedy, we will never
know all the details, but we know that God is suffering
in it all and we can be present to him. In the memorable
words of Dietrich Bonhoeffer, 'Christians stand by God
in his hour of grieving.'[13] He knows there is a limit to
the agony we can absorb from the world and never asks
us to bear more than we are able. But he says to us as
he said to his disciples in the Garden of Gethsemane,
'Stay by me – watch and pray.' He asks us to 'assist him'
by the fidelity of our silence before him. Then it is that
the Holy Spirit will pray and groan in us with a love we
cannot comprehend – a love which will reach down,
through the channels we become, into the depths of the
world's life, and touch with compassion and comfort
those who are in unimaginable anguish.

Men go to God when they are sore bestead,
Pray to him for succour, for his peace, for bread,
For mercy on their sick, sinning or dead;
All men do so, Christian and unbelieving.

Men go to God when he is sore bestead,
Find him poor and scorned, without shelter or
    bread,
Whelmed under weight of the wicked, the weak, the
    dead;
Christians stand by God in his hour of grieving.

God goeth to every man when sore bestead,
Feedeth body and spirit with his bread;
For Christians, pagans alike he hangs dead,
And both alike forgiving.[14]

The Feast of the Sacred Heart is one of the most beautiful and most under-celebrated feasts of the Church. I suspect that one of the reasons why many Protestants have backed off from it (in the past, at least) is because of the associations the very term 'Sacred Heart' has with garish pictures and statues. The figure of Christ is sometimes depicted with a bright red heart superimposed on the breast, either dripping with blood or shining with golden rays. Some of the present statues even have battery-operated hearts that throb with neon lights! But every attempt to represent the Sacred Heart in pictorial terms is doomed to fall short of the meaning of the feast, for how do we encapsulate visually what is nothing less than a celebration of the love of Jesus? It is a feast in which we recount the infinite love of the One who opened his heart upon the cross in utter vulnerability; a feast in which we attempt to express the inexpressible – his love for us and the love-longing that wells up in our hearts in response.

We are completely confounded in these attempts until we allow metaphor, image and symbol to become handmaids of the Lord to us. The reality of the experience of this divine love cannot be conveyed in any other way, but the degree of literalism in the religious art that we can tolerate will vary from individual to individual, and what appealed to one age in history may repel later ages! Metaphor is valuable to us because it

> draws on images from the natural world, from our senses, and from the world of human, social structures, and yokes them to psychological and spiritual realities in such a way that we are left gasping; we have no way to explain fully a metaphor's power, it simply is.[15]

Image, icon and symbol too have a life-force of their own. They convey truth and have converting power where words alone would fail.

All this needs to be recognised when we talk of the Feast of the Sacred Heart. What starts out as an attempt to visualise becomes 'an intuition of the real'. God sends a grace – something we could never have brought about deliberately.

After his account of the death of Jesus, and the piercing of his side, John adds two texts, of which the second is a powerful expression of what he himself had experienced. 'They shall look on him whom they have pierced' (John 19:37).

Through the open wound in the side of Jesus, which he had obviously contemplated deeply throughout the course of his long life, John 'entered into God's secret. And he understood it was love.' Explanations are pointless, so John quickly invites us, too, to contemplate the deep wound in Christ's heart.

People, says Yves Raguin,

have striven to know God by every possible and imaginable means, but the greater number of these efforts have come to nothing. To know God in depth we had to be able to pierce him. This would be possible only if God offered himself to us for piercing. And by becoming human, that is exactly what he did. The cry, 'God is dead, we have killed him' as Nietzsche claimed, is an illusion. We have not killed him, we have only pierced him to the heart. When we pierced him, we peered into his mystery . . . God let us pierce him and we understood he was Love.[16]

As with all the great events in the life of Jesus, we can locate them in a historical and geographical setting (e.g. the baptism, transfiguration, passion, resurrection and ascension), and, at the same time, recognise that they are eternal realities continually working themselves out in every generation of believers.

This is true of the piercing of the side of Jesus – indeed, more than the side, the very heart. For we are told that when the sword pierced him, blood and water flowed forth, indicating that the pericardium had ruptured with the piercing. It holds within it that kind of eternal secret and continuing efficacy.

A prayer picture of the woundedness of Christ

In prayer, God sometimes sends us pictures, sometimes words and sometimes neither. But pictures are a vital part of the language of the heart, as Leanne Payne points out, and can be the means of insight and revelation. One such life-giving picture was given to me some while ago.

I stood at the edge of what seemed like a long narrow chasm. It was night, but some light (possibly from the moon) allowed me to pick out the jagged edges of the chasm and caused the walls – sheer in their descent – to glisten, like a coal face. Down in the very depths something flowed and was occasionally visible from fleeting shafts of light here and there.

Not perhaps a very startling picture, and yet it touched some kind of inner spring that had incredible quickening power. I was drawn back to that abyss each time I came to prayer. Time and time again, I stood on the edge of that chasm, daring every so often to look down into its depths. I knew I had to stay with that picture, remain there teetering on the edge of the abyss. I could do no other, even though it was all very mystifying. It made no sense, yet seemed like a magnet drawing me into a field of spiritual energy.

Whilst I remained puzzled as to why this had been shown to me, from the moment I had seen it there was a strong sense of being drawn into the abyss, a compelling urge to take a plunge into those depths, which was both terrifying and yet magnetic in its attraction. And then the key to the mystery was given to me and I 'saw' that the 'abyss' was a giant-sized picture of the wound in the side of Jesus made by the piercing of the soldier's sword – a wound that was vast and deep in its mystery. In such an experience, there *are* no words. One can only bow before the mystery and seek to yield oneself to it. It was undeniably a call to descend into that abyss and be totally immersed – in love, the love that flowed and ever flows in the depths of Christ's woundedness. And gradually it dawned on me that such an immersion would be a further outworking of my initial baptism, in water, that death by 'drowning' that plunges us into the passion of Christ and leads to resurrection vitality. Obedience to a further immersion in the mystery of God's love would, in some way I could not and cannot comprehend, enable that gaping wound to open on to the hearts of others and, more amazingly still, draw them into the heart of God's blazing love.

Plunging into that abyss reveals more than the mystery of God's love, of course. It also unmasks our own nothingness and need and that, in itself, is a humbling but strangely empowering grace, for it hollows out a greater capacity for his love in us. If it were merely that abyss which is in each of us, we would flee from its anguish and pain. But this one draws us with compelling strength. Whilst writing this chapter I came upon an old Methodist hymn entitled, 'O God, Thou bottomless abyss', the second verse of which speaks poignantly and poetically of this compulsion born of need.

> Unfathomable depths Thou art;
> O plunge me in Thy mercy's sea!
> Void of true wisdom is my heart;
> With love embrace and cover me.[17]

This immersion calls each of us, too, to await a heart's

piercing, to a more fundamental understanding of our baptism and what it means to be 'in Christ', hidden in his heart, continually being dipped in his sorrow, his cleansing and his compassion, till we are changed into a love that will change the world.

For some this immersion has been literal. Manche Masemola's discipleship in the face of her family's fierce opposition led in 1928 to martyrdom. They were determined that this young woman from Sekhukhuneland should not be baptised. 'Perhaps I shall be baptised in my own blood,' she said to her priest – and she was.

Others like Archbishops Jawani Luwum and Oscar Romero, the Jesuit martyrs of El Salvador and Algeria, and countless other martyrs, have also plunged into the abyss of love and been 'baptised' in their own blood as they have responded fully to their baptismal vocation to be totally immersed in the death and resurrection of Jesus. Their sacrificial self-surrender symbolises the undying love of Christ and, in a mysterious way, helps to complete what is lacking in his afflictions (Col. 1:24). They became what St Swithun called 'partners of Christ's pain'.

> O cruel death, O wounds most deep,
> O guiltless blood, O bitter pain,
> Alas! who can forbear to weep to see
> God's Son so cruelly slane.
> O Saviour sweet, hear my request,
> *Make me partner of your pain;*

In solace let me never rest, since Thou
in sorrow dost remain.
And if it be Thy glorious will
that I should taste of this Thy cup,
Lo! here Thy pleasure to fulfil,
Myself I wholly offer up.[18]

SIX

END WITHOUT END
The Goal of All Longing

> He himself is my contemplation.
> He is my delight.
> Him for his own sake
> I seek above me,
> From him himself,
> I feed within me.
> He is the field in which I labour,
> He is the fruit for which I labour.
> He is my cause.
> He is my effect.
> He is my beginning.
> He is my end without end.
> He is for me eternity.

Isaac of Stella[1]

It was 1988, and the Pope was coming to Botswana. For weeks, months and even years, our Roman Catholic friends had been preparing for the visit – planning down to the minutest detail. A papal representative had been several times to check arrangements. Lists were issued of the Pope's every requirement from security coverage down to the menu for his breakfast.

After endless committees, reams of paper, hours of

travelling up and down the country to train choirs and instruct the faithful; after the dancing had been rehearsed, hundreds of new vestments embroidered, chalices gathered from every possible source, tickets printed, car stickers distributed – the great day finally came.

Following a visit to the State House, to meet the President, there was to be a papal audience for priests and members of religious orders. Armed with invitations, special identity cards with their yellow and white ribbons, we set off for the cathedral.

As the building began to fill, the excitement grew almost to fever pitch. Outside, the cheering suddenly soared into a crescendo as the Popemobile came into view. The band was completely drowned by a deafening roar as the Pope dismounted and walked to the West Door.

In those few seconds as we turned to watch his entry, I was suddenly filled with an overwhelming pang, a kind of intense yearning – for the coming of the Lord, himself. If only *he* would walk through that door, that it would be *his* face we would see, *his* voice we would hear, *his* hand we would clasp.

Then my thoughts were shattered, for the small, white-clad figure was now moving up the aisle to a storm of clapping and a barrage of camera flashes. Everyone was smiling. Staid old nuns clambered on to the pews to see better. Then, suddenly, in one swift movement, the Pope was on his knees, deep in prayer. Instantly, the clapping stopped, the clicking of the cameras ceased, nobody jostled to get a better view. We were a group of believers, of one heart and mind, united not only in our desire to see the Pope but in our permanent stance of watching and waiting for the Lord.

Despite the difficulties we have at times in defining or articulating our desires, every so often it is as though we touch a mainspring of our purest of all longings – and it leaps into sharp focus overwhelming us by its sheer power. It is our longing to see the face of God, to behold him who is the source and goal of all our desiring. It is at once a pain and a joy, a fullness and an inner ache.

We can probably all point to such moments of pure longing when it is as though life takes on an extra dimension and vibrates in its contact with reality – and those moments hold within them a creative energy and nourishing power that can stay with us for *years*.

As a teenager, I used to go to summer schools run by a Missionary Society as part of my annual summer holiday. On one occasion, we were taught a beautiful hymn of Indian origin, with a haunting tune. We sang it at evening prayers that night and the chorus stayed with us as we went to bed.

Show me Thy face at the dawn.
Give me to see Thee at break of day, O Saviour King.
Show me Thy face at the dawn.[2]

Little did we realise that the request would be granted quite literally to one of our number. She drowned during our early morning bathing party next day.

But the hymn was not written primarily with death in view but to form part of a communicant's overnight preparation for communion, for that meeting in bread and wine, where we 'touch and handle things unseen'.

Here and now we see God under a veil, in many thousands of guises. Our vision of him is fragmented — a flash of 'knowing' as we glimpse him in creation, in other people, in all the numerous acts of kindness and generosity from unexpected quarters, in the circumstances of our life and the providential coincidences.

> Every 'other' is a new face of the hidden God, a new incarnation of the Christ we seek, a new manifestation of divine creativity. The stranger is a bearer of truth that might not otherwise have been received. Sometimes the 'other' or the 'stranger' is quite near us, even approaching us in people we think we know well, in situations we think we can handle, or the places we take for granted!³

The 'eyes of the heart need to be enlightened' (Ephesians 1:18) if we are to be able thus to locate God in the warp and woof of our dailiness and enlarge our composite picture of his face. All such 'seeing' is the work of the Holy Spirit.

> The Holy Spirit is that power which opens eyes that are closed, hearts that are unaware and minds that shrink from too much reality . . . vision and vulnerability go together.⁴

The fragmented vision

Leo Théron is an artist in stained glass whose studio in Pretoria opened up for me a new dimension of seeing. The draft from which he was working (on yards of kitchen paper which rolled out across the table and down on to the floor) was, to my unpractised eye, a mass of baffling geometrical shapes. Looking at it fairly close-to and in small segments, it was impossible to imagine what the finished work would be like.

Across one work top were scattered hundreds of small pieces of glass, all shapes and colours. The process of piecing them together in lead frames required meticulous precision and endless patience. But even seeing one fragment of the whole window was a tiny foresight, a very partial view, of the final glory.

Standing against a window in one part of the studio, with the sunlight streaming through, was a piece of work he had recently completed – the head of 'Christ in Transfiguration'.[5] It was awesome. I felt I was on holy ground and could only gaze in wonder that those chunky bits of glass (which he had to file, sandpaper and refine) had combined to portray such incredible beauty – a face full of pathos, sorrow, tenderness, love and serenity. But, of course, I was in the workshop of a master craftsman. Only when I was taken to see some of his windows 'in situ' – massive, floor-to-ceiling kaleidoscopes of colour and powerful imagery, filling cathedrals and churches with a rainbow profusion of light – could I begin to grasp what faith and vision he had to have to believe that all that jumble of fragmented glass, pieced together in countless small sections, would one day be fitted into vast frames to make a majestic whole to give a full vision of glory.

That's how it is in our longing to see the face of God. We see him in numerous small ways, but only very partially. He bids us 'gather up the fragments [of our life], that nothing be lost', and discern in them something of his nature and splendour. And as we gradually piece together those fleeting glimpses, he calls us to have faith that the Invisible is becoming a little more visible.

It is part of his infinite mercy that God does not reveal to us too much, too soon. The eyes of our hearts have to be adjusted to his comings. There are certain preconditions. According to Jesus, it is 'the pure in heart' who will ultimately be granted the full vision of God. Whilst any part of us remains 'glued' to the spiders' webs of this world, which cloud our vision, God will withhold further insight. He keeps us waiting, looking and longing until our gaze is purified and free from all self-regard.

If we look carefully at the bottom of this dark labyrinth that is our heart, our consciousness, our past, our present, our impulses towards the future, can we say that we are prepared for a meeting with God? [– a fuller vision of his glory?] Dare we wish for one? Yes – but only in God's good time, as a gift from him; but to will it and to force God to such a meeting – no! It is more than we could bear. And yet, that is how we behave, blinded by the visible,

sightless before the awesome greatness of the Invisible, lacking that sense of wonder, of reverent fear,
of that vision which faith gives, of the humbling
feeling of having touched the hem of the robe of
Christ.[6]

In the words of a much loved hymn:

> Eternal Light! Eternal Light!
> How pure the soul must be,
> When placed within thy searching sight,
> It shrinks not, but with calm delight
> Can live and look on Thee.
> O how can I, whose native sphere
> Is dark, whose mind is dim,
> Before the Ineffable appear,
> And on my naked spirit bear
> The uncreated beam?[7]

The hymn concludes with the assurance that there is a
way for us to come to the point where we may dwell in
the eternal light – through the offering and sacrifice of
Christ and the Holy Spirit's energies.

One of the most undervalued gifts of the Spirit is that
of holy fear, and the consequence of not asking for it is
our eventual trivialisation of God. The danger of losing
the gift is all the greater in an age where familiarity has
replaced formality. For all that the Lord is our beloved
and intimate friend, he is also the King of Glory.

A beautiful description of awe and wonder before
greatness, trembling in reverent fear and longing but

incalculable joy, is found, surprisingly enough, in *Wind in the Willows*.

> 'This is the place of my song-dream, the place the music played to me' whispered the Rat, as if in a trance. 'Here, in this holy place, here if anywhere, surely we shall find Him!' Then suddenly the Mole felt a great Awe fall upon him, an awe that turned his muscles to water, bowed his head, and rooted his feet to the ground. It was no panic terror – indeed, he felt wonderfully at peace and happy – but it was an awe that smote and held him and, without seeing, he knew that it could only mean that some Presence was very, very near. With difficulty he turned to look for his friend, and saw him at his side, cowed, stricken, and trembling violently. And still there was utter silence in the populous, bird-haunted branches around them; and still the light grew and grew.
>
> All this he saw, for one moment breathless and intense, vivid on the morning sky; and still, as he looked, he lived, and still as he lived, he wondered.
>
> 'Rat!' he found breath to whisper, shaking. 'Are you afraid?'
>
> 'Afraid?' murmured the Rat, his eyes shining with unutterable love. 'Afraid! of Him? O, never, never! And yet – and yet – O, Mole I am afraid!'
>
> Then the two animals crouching to the earth, bowed their heads and did worship.[8]

The Psalmist wrote: 'When I awake and see his likeness, I shall be satisfied' (Psalm 16:15), which in literal translation means 'satiated' – full to overflowing, unable to absorb any more. And that is the ultimate bliss we believe will one day be ours.

> When I stand before Him
> I shall see His face.
> And there I'll serve my King forever
> In that holy place.[9]

Keith Green could not have foreseen, as he wrote those words, how soon he would be standing before the Lord and seeing his face, for very shortly after, he and two of his children were killed in a plane crash. But his hymn lives on and has voiced for us the sure and certain hope that we have as believers.

'Seek not an experience of me,' says the Lord. 'Seek my face.' And in the end, we shall no longer yearn after God as starving animals long for food, but will sink to our knees before him in worship, as those who are gorged, satiated. *That* is the horizon to which we travel, that is our goal and our journey's end, for which this life is part of our preparation. That will be the joy of the Beatific Vision. The little foretastes we see in this life only serve to whet our appetites for more and more. For, in this life, 'really to see God is never to have had one's fill of desiring him'.[10]

What metaphor can we use to describe what we believe that moment of vision will be like? F. W. Faber attempts it as he talks of the rapture it will be to lie prostrate before the throne of God, in unlimited leisure, and gaze and gaze on him.[11]

St John in the Apocalypse sees the whole company of heaven (myriads and myriads of them) surrounding the throne of God in worship, singing in full voice: 'Worthy is the Lamb that was slain, to receive power, and wisdom and wealth and might and honour and glory and blessing . . . for ever and ever' – at which the elders fell down and worshipped (Revelation 5:11–14).

We *can* only imagine heaven in terms of the high moments in worship and wonder that we experience here and now – magnified to an extreme. But not everyone gets excited at the image of being prostrate in worship for eternity. And, indeed, heaven is not a static state. It is 'endless growth in divine beauty, the face of God transforming us more and more into his likeness'.[12] It is a continual rebirthing of love, for the Source and Goal of all our longing is the One who is himself holy love and wholly love, who assures us that we are precious in his sight, honoured and loved. Our 'end without end' will not be simply 'to arrive' but a continuing growth and movement towards becoming, to greater, purer love and ever expanding freedom.

> Nothing in this world is truly motionless, and I suspect nothing in the next world is either. We human beings think in terms of perfect ends, but I doubt that God thinks that way. I have a hunch that God has a lot more to do with tender beginnings than with efficient ends.[13]

When stripped of all our protective barriers, we yield to the invitation of love without reserve and begin to open up and reach out. Then the immense freedom it gives can be the source of endless beginnings. We have so often been surprised by love, graced moments that illuminate the dailiness of life. But the greatest surprise is yet to come. Prayer is a coming home, and the many little homecomings prepare us for that greater Homecoming when, released from our addictions, beyond the need of symbols and images, we encounter our End without End, the one who is for us – eternity. For it is he who meets us every day who will meet us at the end, even Jesus Christ, our Lord. And as we stand before him in that holy place, 'we shall rest and we shall see; we shall see and we shall love; we shall love and we shall praise; behold what will be in the end without end! For what is our end but to reach the Kingdom which has no end.'[14]

SEVEN

A QUARRY OF QUOTATIONS
Midwife to our Longings

Of all the many ways of entering into contemplative prayer (and if we have made a space for God in our lives and seek to commune with him, then we are all contemplatives – it is not a specialist field), the words and wisdom of pilgrims, past and present, can often be most helpful.

As this book has maintained, there are longings hidden within each of us which maybe have been gestating over many years, that need to be brought to birth, owned and named. This quarry of quotations is offered as a midwife to do that – for at least some. It is not a chapter to be read through at speed. Each quotation needs to be pondered. Some may help in the birthing, others will not.

If none do, that is all right. You may like to begin to collect words that do speak to you and begin your own anthology. It may be an anthology of words or visual symbols and images.

Keeping an anthology can become a very helpful map of our spiritual journey. As we look back in our notes and see what spoke to us in the months and years past, it is possible to see where we have travelled and perhaps moved on. But just as we celebrate birthdays and give thanks for the gift of life, so when we consider what it was that brought to birth some of our longings, we are led into thanksgiving and renewed joy. At times, we are taken back to our 'first love' and spiritual energy and zest are rekindled.

Often the midwife to our longings is another person – who by the quality of listening that they offer, or by an almost 'throwaway' remark can suddenly bring forth the longing in an identifiable shape and form. We are fortunate indeed in such encounters when the Holy Spirit is clearly at work.

The following quotations are a mixture of many strands of spirituality and have been culled from my own Quotation Books kept over many years, and from other sources.

Desire

Lord, I desire, I desire,
I cannot say how much.
I only know I stand in need of all things,
And would that my desire were as great as is my need!
Lord, who alone canst satisfy the human heart's desire,
And fill with all Thy fullness the abyss of human need,
Hear now how I desire all good things,
And Thee, Thyself, my God, above all else,
Who givest all.

A Fratre Scripta[1]

Ere ever I cried to Thee, Thou, Most Merciful
had'st called and sought me that I might find Thee
and finding love Thee. Even so I sought and

117

found Thee, O Lord, and desire to love Thee.
Increase my desire, bestow Thyself upon me, my
   God.
Yield Thee unto me, see I love Thee but too little;
strengthen my love. Let love to Thee alone influence
my heart and let the thought of Thee be all my joy.

St Augustine

Jesus receive my heart, and bring me to Thy love:
all my desire Thou art, and Thy coming I covet.
Make me clean from sin, and let us never part:
Kindle fire within me, that I may win to Thy love,
and see Thy face, Jesus, in bliss which shall never
   cease.

Richard Rolle[2]

Thou art He whom I have sought,
When shall I see Thy face?
Do Thou make my soul clean.
Thy love changeth the look on me.

Richard Rolle[3]

Set thy heart upon him, who sets his upon thee;
seek him who hast so solicitously sought thee;
whose Goodness hath prevented thee, and is the cause
   of thine.
he is the Merit, he the Reward, he the Fruit and the
   End of thy love.

St Augustine[4]

118

For myself, I have only one desire, the desire for
solitude to disappear into God, to be submerged in
his peace, to be lost in the secret of his face.

Thomas Merton[5]

Whom have I in heaven but you?:
and there is no one . . . I desire in comparison with
you.

Psalm 73:25

For giving me desire,
An eager thirst, a burning ardent fire,
A virgin infant flame,
A love with which into the world I came,
An inward hidden heavenly love,
Which in my soul did work and move,
And ever, ever me inflame,
With restless longing heavenly avarice,
That never could be satisfied,
That did incessantly a Paradise
Unknown suggest, and something undescried
Discern, and bear me to it; be
Thy name for ever prais'd by me.

Thomas Traherne[6]

For one whose heart is aflame with love, the world
appears to be the very countenance of God.

Louis Lavelle[7]

O Thou who comest from above
The pure celestial fire to impart,
Kindle a flame of sacred love
On the mean altar of my heart.

There let it for Thy glory burn
With inextinguishable blaze,
And trembling to its source return
With humble prayer and fervent gaze.

Jesus confirm my heart's desire
To work and speak and think for Thee.
Still let me guard the holy fire
And still stir up Thy gift in me.

Ready for all Thy perfect will
My acts of faith and love repeat,
Till death Thine endless mercies seal
And make the sacrifice complete.

Charles Wesley

Jesu, Thou joy of loving hearts!
Thy fount of life, Thou light of men!
From the best bliss that earth imparts
We turn unfilled to Thee again.

Thy truth unchanged hath ever stood;
Thou savest those who on thee call;
To them that seek Thee thou art good;
To those who find thee all in all.

We taste thee, O thou living Bread,
And long to feast upon thee still;
We drink of thee, the fountain-head,
And thirst our souls from thee to fill.

Our restless spirits yearn for thee,
Where'er our changeful lot is cast,
Glad when thy gracious smile we see,
Blest when our faith can hold thee fast.

O Jesu, ever with us stay;
Make all our moments calm and bright;
Chase the dark night of sin away;
Shed o'er the world thy holy light.

Twelfth-century Latin hymn[8]

Lord,
you know our deepest desires
and we know the vision of your Kingdom . . .
we bring before you those elements in our lives
in need of your transforming power:
that which we misuse or neglect,
that which we most reluctantly let go of,
that which we believe is not good enough:
inspire us and disturb us to examine our deepest
    desires.
Prepare us for your way, O Lord
Your kingdom come, your will be done . . .

But if we have turned in upon our emptiness
refused the risks you require of us

121

idolised our self-sufficiency
and clung to our captivity
have mercy on us,
God who wrestles and embraces us
shatter our illusions
refuse your comfort of angels
feed our hope and our hunger
with the adventurous faith
of your spirit
until grace is our only sufficiency
Amen.

The Pattern of our Days[9]

... For this cause was your side pierced that an
entrance might be opened for us ... Why have you
been wounded again? That through the visible
wound we might see the invisible wound of love ...
Who is there who would not love this wounded
Heart? Who would not return love for love to him
that has loved so well?

St Bonaventure[10]

As long as you will it, I shall remain with my gaze
fixed on you, for I long to be fascinated by your
divine eyes, to be prey to your love.

St Thérèse of Lisieux[11]

When by his Grace our courteous Lord shows
himself to our soul, then we have what we desire
and for the time see nothing more to pray for but

all our mind and strength is gathered up in the sight of him. This is a high, unimaginable prayer in my sight.

Julian of Norwich[12]

Reveal your presence
And let the vision of your beauty kill me.
Behold, the malady
of love is incurable
Except in your presence and
before your face.

St John of the Cross[13]

My beloved is the mountains,
The solitary wooded valleys,
The strange islands,
The raging torrents,
The whisper of the amorous breezes.
The tranquil night
As the approaches of dawn,
The silent music,
The murmuring solitude,
The supper which revives and enkindles love.

St John of the Cross[14]

Becoming the Beloved is the great spiritual journey we have to make. Augustine's words 'My soul is restless until it rests in you, O God' captures well this journey. I know that the fact that I am always searching for God, always struggling to discover the

123

fullness of love, always yearning for the complete truth, tells me that I have already been given a taste of God, of Love and of Truth. I can only look for something that I have, to some degree, already found. How can I search for beauty and truth unless that beauty and truth are already known to me in the depth of my heart? It seems that all of us human beings have deep inner memories of the paradise that we have lost. Maybe the word 'innocence' is better than the word 'paradise'. We were innocent before we started feeling guilty; we were in light before we entered into darkness; we were at home before we started to search for a home. Deep in the recesses of our minds and hearts there lies hidden the treasure we seek. We know its precariousness, and we know that it holds the gift we most desire: a life stronger than death.

Henri J. M. Nouwen[15]

Remember: the simple desire for God is already the beginning of faith. Leading to eternal life, the trust of faith has a beginning but will have no end.

Brother Roger of Taizé[16]

He is the Life I want to live,
He is the Light that I want to radiate,
He is the Way to the Father.
He is the Love with which I want to love,
He is the Joy that I want to share,
He is the Peace that I want to sow,

Jesus is Everything to me.
Without him, I can do nothing.

Mother Teresa[17]

It often happens that we are unable to say a single word to God; we only wish his closeness, we only want to be beside him. Peace pervades us and we feel reborn.

Waltraud Herbstrith[18]

God and the person meet like lovers who can be close to each other more by keeping silence than by speaking.

Waltraud Herbstrith[19]

Be thou my vision, beloved Lord: none other is aught but the King of the seven heavens.

Be thou my meditation by day and night: may it be thou that I behold ever in my sleep.

Be thou my speech: be thou my understanding: be thou for me: may I be for thee.

Be thou my father: may I be thy son: mayst thou be mine: may I be thine.

Be thou alone my special love: let there be none other save the High-King of Heaven.

Thy love in my soul and in my heart – grant this to me, O King of the seven heavens.

Beloved Christ, what'er befall me, O Ruler of all,
be thou my vision.

Celtic traditional (eight century)[20]

To Thee we tread the road that Christ has trod,
So rest our hearts in Him: Thy Heart, dear God.

John Randal Bradburne[21]

O happy the soul that is drawn by grace to God, so
that, through the unity of the Spirit in God, it takes
no thought of itself, loving none but God and loving
itself only in God.

This is the end, this is the consummation, perfection, peace, the joy of God, the joy in the Holy
Spirit, this is Silence in Heaven.

William of Saint Thierry

Be willing to be blind, and give up all longing to
know the why and how, for knowing will be more
of a hindrance than a help. It is enough that you
should feel moved lovingly by you know not what,
and that in this inward urge you have no real thought
for anything less than God, and that your desire is
steadily and simply turned towards him.

The Cloud of Unknowing[22]

So if you are to stand and not fall, never give up your
firm intention: beat away at this cloud of unknowing
between you and God with that sharp dart of longing
love. Hate to think about anything less than God.

The Cloud of Unknowing[23]

God . . . is found when He is sought and when He is no longer sought He escapes us. He is heard only when we hope to hear Him, and if, thinking our hope to be fulfilled, we cease to listen, He ceases to speak. His silence ceases to be vivid and becomes dead, even though we recharge it with the echo of our own emotional noise.

Thomas Merton[24]

Prayer is then not just a formula of words, or a series of desires springing up in the heart – it is the orientation of the whole body, mind and spirit to God in silence, attention and adoration. All good meditative prayer is a conversion of our entire self to God.

Thomas Merton[25]

Some time ago a poor young Indian girl lay seriously ill in a Calcutta hospital. She knew that she was not likely to recover, but she was not afraid. One afternoon she had lain quite still, with her eyes shut, and for so long that the nurse came to see if she was all right. The girl opened her eyes. Had she been asleep? asked the nurse. 'No,' said the girl, 'I was praying.' 'What were you asking God for, to make you well?' asked the nurse. 'No, I wasn't asking for anything, I was just loving him.'

John Carden[26]

Give me a true perception of things unseen, and

make me truly, practically, and in the details of my life, prefer you to anything on earth. Give me a true instinct determining between right and wrong, humility in all things, and a tender, longing love of you.

John Henry Newman

For what do we understand by loving God save that our souls are wholly occupied with him and that our one and only desire is to enjoy the vision of God.

Julianus Pomerius (fifth century)

We ascend to the heights of contemplation by the steps of everyday life.

Gregory the Great (sixth century)

And so the yearning strong,
with which the soul will long,
shall far outpass the power of human telling;
for none can guess its grace, till he become the place
wherein the Holy Spirit makes his dwelling.

Bianco di Siena (see *Hymns Old and New*, No. 96, v.4)[27]

The peak of love's ecstasy is to long for God's contentment, not our own; is to gratify, not our own wishes, but God's.

St Francis de Sales[28]

There are times when the soul neither hears its beloved, nor speaks to him, nor feels any indication of his presence; it simply knows that it is in God's presence, that is where it wants to be.

St Francis de Sales[29]

For the darkness of loving
in which it is safe to surrender
to let go of our self-protection
and to stop holding back our desire,
we praise you, O God:

for the darkness and the light
are both alike to you.

Janet Morley[30]

NOTES

Chapter 1: DEEP CALLS TO DEEP

1 Psalm 42:7.

2 William Wordsworth, 'Ode: Intimations of Immortality' V in *Wordsworth: Poetical Works*, ed. Thomas Hutchinson (Oxford University Press, 1969), p. 460.

3 Augustine, Confessions I. 1.

4 Gregory of Nyssa, cited by K. Norris in *The Cloister Walk* (New York: Riverhead Books, 1996), p. 127.

5 Anne Frank, *The Diary of Anne Frank* (Pan, 1968), p. 130.

6 Source forgotten.

7 Richard Bach, cited by Ronald Rolheiser in *Forgotten among the Lilies* (Spire, 1990), p. 245.

8 Ronald Rolheiser, op. cit., p. 13.

9 James Finley, *Merton's Palace of Nowhere* (Ave Maria Press, 1978), p. 149.

10 Sr Janet CSMV, Hymn for the Feast of the Sacred Heart (from which the title of this book has been adapted), Daily Office Part 2. Copyright CSMV.

11 Ronald Rolheiser, op. cit., p. 19.

12 Ronald Rolheiser, op. cit., p. 5.

13 James Finley, op. cit., p. 47.

14 Wendy Beckett, *The Gaze of Love* (Marshall Pickering, 1994), p. 58.

15 Augustine, Treatise on the Letter of John, 4.6, cited in John Burnaby, *Amor Dei* (The Canterbury Press, Norwich, 1997), p. 97.

16 Bertrand Russell, reference unknown.

17 James Finley, op. cit., p. 61.

18 Quotations in the following three paragraphs are from Leanne Payne, *The Healing Presence* (Kingsway, 1989), p. 133.

19 *Epektasis*: a straining forward, the noun derived from the same verb
    that St Paul used in Philippians 3:13 where he speaks of 'straining
    forward to what lies ahead', implying a reaching out to possesss
    the Unpossessable, eagerly stretching and yearning in desire, ever
    growing and deepening in love for God.

20 Rowan Williams, *The Wound of Knowledge* (DLT, 1979), p. 60, com-
    menting on Gregory of Nyssa, *The Life of Moses*.

21 Adapted from St Bernard, *On the Love of God*, XI. 33, cited by Rowan
    Williams, op. cit., p. 112.

22 From *Sayings of the Desert Fathers*, cited by Joan Chittister in *Wisdom
    Distilled from the Daily* (HarperCollins San Francisco, 1991), p. 53.

23 Richard Rolle, *The Fire of Love* (Methuen, 1920), p. 185.

24 Anon., *The Cloud of Unknowing*, trans. Clifton Wolters (Penguin, 1961),
    ch. 2.

25 Yves Raguin SJ, *The Depth of God*, ed. Edward Malatesta SJ, Volume 10
    (Anthony Clarke, 1979), pp. 108–109.

26 Wendy Beckett, op. cit., p. 62.

27 Anon., *The Cloud of Unknowing*, ed. Evelyn Underhill (J. M. Watkins,
    1912), ch. 2.

28 Abhishiktananda, *Guru and Disciple*, trans. Heather Sandeman (SPCK,
    1974), pp. 99–100.

Chapter 2: WEBS OF ILLUSION

1 Gregory of Nyssa, *Commentary on the Psalms*. Cited by Thomas Merton
   The Ascent of Truth (London: Hollis and Carter, 1951), pp. 17–18.

2 Ibid. (bracketed words added).

3 Thomas Merton, *The Ascent of Truth*, pp. 19–20.

4 James Houston, *The Heart's Desire* (Lion, 1992), p. 57.

5 Ibid., p. 57.

6 Ibid., p. 57.

7 Ibid., p. 58.

8 Gerald May, *The Awakened Heart* (HarperCollins, 1991), p. 106.

9 Cited by Eric Voegelin in *Immortality, Experience and Symbol*, and quoted
   by James Houston, op. cit., p. 12.

10 Joan Puls, *Seek Treasures in Small Fields* (DLT, 1993), p. 142.

11 Ronald Rolheiser, *Forgotten among the Lilies*, op. cit., p. 190.

12 *Metanoia* – the Greek word for a complete turning round, a conver-
    sion, a change of heart.

Notes

13 Margaret Smith, *The Way of the Mystics* (Sheldon Press, 1976), p. 6.

14 Gerald May, op. cit., adapted from jacket blurb.

15 Ibid.

16 Ibid.

17 I am indebted to Gerald May for this insight from the Hebrew, op. cit., p. 93.

18 Ibid., p. 93.

19 Ibid., p. 97.

20 Etty Hillesum, *An Interrupted Life* (New York: HarperCollins, 1990), pp. 133–134.

21 Ibid.

22 Quoted by Archbishop Desmond Tutu in *Prophetic Witness in South Africa*, ed. Leonard Hulley, Louise Kretzschmer & Luke Pato (Cape Town, Pretoria, Johannesburg: Human and Rousseau, 1996), p. 40.

23 Andrew Meier, Richard Ostling, Andrew Purvis, *Time*, 7 April 1997, pp. 33–34. I am indebted to these reporters for almost all of the cultic detail and their views of the contemporary scene in the USA in this section of the chapter.

24 Stephen O'Leary, *Arguing the Apocalypse*, quoted by the above reporters in their article in *Time*, 7 April 1997.

25 *Church Times*, 11 April 1997, p. 14.

26 Miguel de Unamuno, cited by James Houston in *The Heart's Desire*, p. 28.

Chapter 3: TEARS ARE MY FOOD

1 Teresa of Avila, *The Interior Castle*, Fourth Mansion, 1.6 (New York: Paulist Press, 1979).

2 Igumen Chariton of Valamo, *The Art of Prayer, An Orthodox Anthology* (Faber & Faber, 1966), p. 63.

3 I am here identifying the 'woman who was a sinner' of Luke 7, with Mary Magdalen, as I did in *Transformed by Love* (DLT, 1989), even though I know many scholars dispute this.

4 John of the Cross; cf. his poem in the final chapter of this book, p. 123.

5 Philip Sheldrake, *Befriending our Desires* (DLT, 1994), p. 32.

6 Eugene Peterson, 'The Contemplative Pastor' in *Christianity Today* (1989), pp. 98ff.

7 Ibid., p. 99.

Notes

8   Ibid., p. 99.

9   A member of the Society of St John the Evangelist, Cowley. Printed by CSMV, Wantage, 1920.

10 Philip Sheldrake, op. cit., p. 41.

11 Source untraced.

12 Dom Vitalis Lehodey OCR, The Ways of Mental Prayer (Dublin: Gill, 1960), Part 3, chap ix, para 2.

13 James Borst, A Method of Contemplative Prayer (Asian Trading Corporation, 1973), p. 17.

14 Anon., The Cloud of Unknowing, trans. Clifton Wolters (Penguin, 1977), ch. 6.

15 Kathleen Norris, A Cloister Walk (New York: Riverhead Books, 1996), p. 133.

16 Rabbi Mendel of Vorki. Reference untraced.

17 Lent, Holy Week and Easter: Services and Prayers (Church House Publishing/ Cambridge University Press/SPCK, 1984), p. 45.

18 Alan Jones, The Drama of the Spiritual Journey: An Exploration of Dante's Divine Comedy (Atlanta, Georgia: Catacomb Cassettes, 1980).

19 George Maloney, Prayer of the Heart (Notre Dame, Indiana: Ave Maria Press, 1981), p. 87.

20 Thomas Merton, Sign of Jonas (Burns and Oates, 1961), p. 173.

21 James Houston, The Heart's Desire (Lion, 1992), p. 198.

22 Ronald Rolheiser, Forgotten among the Lilies (Spire, 1991), p. 284.

23 John Climacus, The Ladder of Divine Ascent, trans. Lazarus Moore (Faber & Faber, 1959), p. 114.

24 Gregory of Nyssa, De Beatitudine, 3, cited by George Maloney, op. cit., p. 89.

25 Henri Nouwen, Love in a Fearful Land (1986), cited by Ronald Rolheiser, op. cit., p. 283.

26 George Maloney, op. cit., p. 102.

Chapter 4: NEVER SATISFIED

1   Maria Boulding, The Coming of God (Fount Paperbacks, 1984), p. 8.

2   Gregory of Nyssa, Life of Moses, trans. A. J. Malherbe and E. Ferguson, Classics of Western Spirituality (Paulist Press, 1978), pp. 115–116.

3   Gregory the Great, Gospel Homilies; homily for the Feast of St Mary Magdalen (22 July), from the Roman Breviary.

4   James Houston, The Heart's Desire (Lion, 1992), p. 204.

Notes

5 Bernard of Clairvaux, cited by E. Herman in *The Meaning and Value of Mysticism* (James Clarke, 1915), p. 187.

6 James Houston, op. cit., p. 205.

7 Gregory of Nyssa, Homily 5 on the Song of Songs.

8 Thomas Merton, *Thoughts in Solitude* (Burns and Oates, 1958), p. 96.

9 Basil Hume, *Searching for God* (Hodder and Stoughton, 1977), p. 141.

10 Margaret Magdalen, *Jesus, Man of Prayer* (Hodder and Stoughton, 1987), pp. 151–154.

11 Alan Ereira, *The Heart of the World* (Jonathan Cape, 1990), p. 130.

12 George Maloney, *Singers of the New Song* (Ave Maria Press, 1985), p. 59.

13 Anthony Bloom, *Meditations: A Spiritual Journey through the Parables* (Dimension Books, 1971), pp. 28–29.

14 Annie Dillard, *Pilgrim at Tinker's Creek* (New York, 1975), p. 269.

15 Gregory of Nyssa, *Life of Moses*, op. cit., p. 114, para: 231.

16 Kathleen Norris, *A Cloister Walk* (New York: Riverhead Books, 1996), p. 113.

17 Bernard of Clairvaux, 'Jesu, thou joy of loving hearts', trans. R. Palmer, *Hymns Ancient and Modern* (Revised), No. 387.

18 A. W. Tozer, *The Pursuit of God* (Tyndale House Publishers), p. 15.

19 Ronald Rolheiser, *Forgotten among the Lilies*, op. cit., p. 5.

20 George Appleton, *The Oxford Book of Prayer* (OUP, 1985), No. 148, p. 56.

Chapter 5: THE WOUND OF LOVE

1 Sr Janet CSMV, Hymn for the Feast of the Sacred Heart, Daily Office Part 2. Copyright CSMV.

2 Seventeenth-century translation from the Latin; see *English Hymnal*, No. 413.

3 Lawrence Housman, 'A Prayer for Healing of the Wounds of Christ', *Oxford Book of Mystical Verse* (OUP), p. 494.

4 Gale D. Webbe, *The Night and Nothing* (San Francisco: Harper & Row, 1983), pp. 61–62.

5 Tony Campolo, cited by David Runcorn in *Rumours of Life* (DLT, 1996), p. 92.

6 Trevor Hudson, Methodist Minister, retreat conductor, author of *Signposts to Spirituality*.

7 Gerald May, *The Awakened Heart* (HarperCollins, 1991) p. 237.

8 Gerald May, ibid.

9 Charles Péguy, *The Mystery of the Holy Innocents*.

10 Gerald May, op. cit., p. 239.

11 Gerald May, op. cit., p. 240.

12 Meister Eckhart, quoted by Matthew Fox (ed.) in *Illuminations of Hildegard of Bingen* (Santa Fe: Bear & Co., 1985), p. 24.

13 I first heard W. H. Vanstone speak about this at a retreat for CSMV Oblates at St Mary's Convent, Wantage. He also introduced us to the poem by Dietrich Bonhoeffer.

14 Dietrich Bonhoeffer, 'Christians and Pagans', *Letters and Papers from Prison* (The Enlarged Edition, SCM Press, 1997).

15 Kathleen Norris, *A Cloister Walk* (New York: Riverhead Books, 1996), p. 156.

16 Yves Raguin SJ, *Depth of God*, op. cit., pp. 132–133.

17 E. Lange, trans. John Wesley, *Redemption Hymnal*, No. 116.

18 St Swithun Well. St Swithun died in 862. An Anglo-Saxon ecclesiastic, he was adviser to Egbert and made Bishop of Winchester in 852. Details of the source of this particular poem could not be traced.

Chapter 6: END WITHOUT END

1 Isaac of Stella, in *Isaac de l'Étoile, Sermons* 1, ed. A. Hoste and G. Salet (Paris: Sources Chrétienes, 1967), Sermon 5, pp. 122–127.

2 'Show me Thy face at the dawn', *Hymns for Today* (Carey Press), No. 115.

3 Parker J. Palmer, *The Company of Strangers*, cited by Joan Puls, op. cit., p. 64, pp. 101 and 105.

4 John V. Taylor, *The Go-Between God* (SCM Press, 1972), p. 19.

5 Commissioned by the Diocese of Pretoria as a retirement gift to Archbishop Desmond Tutu.

6 Anthony Bloom, *Meditations on the Parables* (Dimension Books, 1971), p. 29.

7 T. Binnery, 'Eternal Light! Eternal Light!' *Redemption Hymnal*, No. 60.

8 Kenneth Graham, *Wind in the Willows* (Methuen & Co. Ltd, [1908] 1951), pp. 166–167.

9 Keith Green, 'There is a Redeemer', *Songs of Fellowship*, No. 544.

10 Gregory of Nyssa, *Life of Moses*, op. cit., pp. 115–116.

11 F. W. Faber, 'My God how wonderful Thou art', *English Hymnal*, No. 441.

12 CSMV, from the Office in Chapel after the Death of a Sister.
13 Gerald May, *The Awakened Heart*, op. cit., p. 34.
14 Augustine, *The City of God*, Book XXII, ch. 30.

Chapter 7: A QUARRY OF QUOTATIONS

1 Printed by the Community of St Mary the Virgin, Wantage, 1920.
2 J. M. Watkins (ed.), *Richard Rolle: Minor Works* (Methuen, 1920), p. 72.
3 Ibid., p. 73.
4 St Augustine, *Meditations*, trans. George Stanhope 1701, 4th edition, 1745, p. 272.
5 Thomas Merton, *The Sign of Jonas* (Hollis and Carter, 1953), p. 16.
6 Thomas Traherne, 'Desire', *Selected Poems and Prose* (Penguin, 1991).
7 Louis Lavelle, *The Meaning of Holiness* (Burns & Oates, 1951), p. 42.
8 *Jesu dulcedo cordium*, trans. R. Palmer (*Hymns Ancient and Modern Revised*, No. 387).
9 Kathy Galloway (ed.), *The Pattern of our Days: Liturgies and Resources for Worship* (Wild Goose Publications, 1996), pp. 123 and 37.
10 *Prayers for the Sacred Heart*, revised edition (Catholic Truth Society).
11 Michael Hollings (ed. and intro.), *By Love Alone* (DLT, 1986).
12 Translation taken from *Enfolded in Love: Daily Readings with Julian of Norwich* (DLT, 1980), p. 24.
13 Taken from *Lamps of Fire*, ed. and intro. Sister Elizabeth Ruth ODC (DLT, 1985).
14 Ibid.
15 Henri J. M. Nouwen, *Life of the Beloved* (Hodder and Stoughton, 1992).
16 Mother Teresa and Brother Roger, *Prayer: Seeking the Heart of God* (Fount Paperbacks, 1991).
17 Mother Teresa, *Our Hearts Full of Love*, ed. Josè Luis Gonzàlez-Balado (Fount Paperbacks, 1989).
18 Waltraud Herbstrith, *In Search of God* (New York: New City Press, 1977).
19 Ibid.
20 A. M. Allchin and Esther de Waal (eds. and introd.), *Threshold of Light* (DLT, 1986).
21 John Dove SJ, *Strange Vagabond of God* (Poolbeg Press Ltd, 1983).
22 *The Cloud of Unknowing*, trans. Clifton Wolters (Penguin, 1978).
23 Ibid.
24 Thomas Merton, *The Sign of Jonas*.

Notes

25 Ibid.
26 John Carden, *Another Day: Prayers of the Human Family* (Triangle/SPCK, 1986).
27 Bianco di Siena (d.1434), trans. R. F. Littledale; see, e.g., *Hymns Old and New*, No. 96, verse 4.
28 Cited in Joseph F. Power OSFS (ed. and introd.), *Finding God Wherever You Are* (New York: New City Press, 1993), p. 92.
29 Ibid., p. 93.
30 Janet Morley, from a litany 'For the darkness of waiting' in *All Desires Known*, expanded edition (SPCK, 1992) p. 58.